DO THE GODS WEAR CAPES?

New Directions in Religion and Literature

Series Editors: Mark Knight, Roehampton University and
Emma Mason, University of Warwick

This series aims to showcase new work at the forefront of religion
and literature through short studies written by leading and rising
scholars in the field. Books will pursue a variety of theoretical
approaches as they engage with writing from different religious and
literary traditions. Collectively, the series will offer a timely critical
intervention to the interdisciplinary crossover between religion and
literature, speaking to wider contemporary interests and mapping
out new directions for the field in the early twenty-first century.

Titles in the series include:

The New Atheist Novel: Fiction, Philosophy and Polemic after 9/11
    Arthur Bradley and Andrew Tate

Blake. Wordsworth. Religion.
    Jonathan Roberts

DO THE GODS WEAR CAPES?

SPIRITUALITY, FANTASY, AND SUPERHEROES

BEN SAUNDERS

continuum

Continuum International Publishing Group
The Tower Building   80 Maiden Lane
11 York Road   Suite 704
London, SE1 7NX   New York, NY 10038

www.continuumbooks.com

British Library Cataloguing-in-Publication Data
A catalogue record for this book is available from the British Library.

ISBN: 978-0-8264-35569 (hardcover)
978-0-8264-41980 (paperback)

Library of Congress Cataloging-in-Publication Data
A catalog record for this book is available from the Library of Congress.

Typeset by Newgen Imaging Systems Pvt Ltd, Chennai, India
Printed and bound in India

For Larisa.

CONTENTS

SERIES EDITORS' PREFACE

This series of short monographs seeks to develop the long-established relationship between the disciplines of religion and literature. We posit that the two fields have always been intimately related, aesthetically, formally and theoretically, creating a reciprocal critical awareness framed by the relatively recent theo-literary thinking of figures such as Walter Benjamin, Martin Buber, Hans-Georg Gadamer, and Geoffrey Hartman. Committed to reflecting on the question of how these two disciplines continue to interact, we are particularly concerned to redress the marked evasion of this relationship within existing scholarship. As Stanley Fish recently declared, religion has the capacity to "succeed high theory and race, gender and class as the centre of intellectual energy in academe." The books in this series are written by a group of critics eager to contribute to and read work intimate with both evolving and new religious and literary debates. Pursuing a variety of theoretical approaches to an array of literary and cultural texts, each study showcases new work on religion and literature while also speaking to wider contemporary concerns with politics, art, and philosophy. In doing so, the books collectively map out new directions for the field in the early twenty-first century.

Mark Knight
Emma Mason

ACKNOWLEDGMENTS

I would like to express my gratitude to the faculty, staff and graduate students at the University of Oregon who contributed to the success of the "Understanding Superheroes" conference, held on October 23 and 24, 2009, and the exhibition, "Faster Than A Speeding Bullet: The Art of the Superhero," which ran from September 26, 2009 to January 3, 2010, at the Jordan Schnitzer Museum of Art—two wonderful events that provided me with opportunities to develop some of the ideas in this book. My heartfelt thanks to: Lisa Abia-Smith, Barbara Altmann, Judith Baskin, Doug Blandy, Stacy De Hart, Karen Ford, Larry Fong, James Fox, Lisa Freinkel, Rick Gehrke, Andrea Gilroy, Andrew Grace, Jill Hartz, Richard Herskowitz, Erick Hoffman, Sharon Kaplan, Kom Konyosying, Kurt Neugebauer, Ken O'Connell, Josh Plencner, Gretchen Ranger, Marilyn Reid, Stephen Rust, Deidre Sandvick, Carter Soles, Carol Stabile, Lauren Suveges, Connie Tapp, Lexy Wellman, Jenee Wilde, and Debbie Williamson-Smith. I'm privileged to know you as colleagues, and proud to call many of you friends.

I'm also grateful to the comic book creators and art collectors I met in the course of developing those projects: Mike Allred, Laura Allred, Marc Andreyko, Brian Michael Bendis, Kurt Busiek, Howard Chaykin, Steve Duin, Danny Fingeroth, Stephen Fishler, Matt Fraction, Michael T. Gilbert, Darrell Grimes, Jeff Harnett, Don Hilliard, Marc Kardell, David Mandel, Tony Marine, Jen Van Meter, Ethan Roberts, Greg Rucka, Stuart Sayger, Diana Schutz, Gail Simone, Vicki Sheridan, Hisako Sugiyama-Fisher, and Vincent Zurzolo. Thank you all for being so generous with your time, and in many cases, your valuable art. (And to Mike and Laura, redoubled thanks for the quite literally awesome cover!)

ACKNOWLEDGMENTS

The Office of the Vice President for Research and Graduate Studies helped with a research stipend for the summer of 2010; I sincerely thank the members of the selection committee for their faith in my work.

Lara Bovilsky, Matt Fraction, Charles Hatfield, Greg Rucka, Paul Peppis, and Richard Stein all read portions of the manuscript in rough draft. Y'all are my real-life heroes. Your encouragement has meant more than you can know, and your comments have saved me embarrassment. Likewise, To The League of Extraordinary Bagelmen—Rick Colby, Justin Field, Jim Thomas, and Paul Qualtere-Burcher — for reading my work and feeding my soul. I look forward to many more breakfasts with you all.

Special shout-outs to: Emma Mason and Mark Knight, for the opportunity; Colleen Coalter and Anna Fleming for your efficiency and patience; Harry Wonham, for believing in me; Ralph C. Wood, for early encouragement; Ken Alder, for sharing the fruits of his own research (everyone reading this should go out and buy *The Lie Detectors* right away); Jean Cottell, Kyle DeBord and Rich Gaston for keeping me on the straight and narrow; my Grandma, for buying me my first comic when I was six years old; my Mum and Dad, for looking after my collection during my itinerant years; and my dazzling daughter Bronwyn, who fortunately does not yet know the power she has over my heart.

Finally, I thank my beautiful wife, Larisa Devine. No dedication could convey my gratitude for your presence in my life. I wish I could love you like a superhero—but fortunately, you seem content to make do with the love of an all-too-ordinary man. For this, I praise the Gods and Goddesses, with and without capes.

INTRODUCTION: THE POWER OF LOVE

1

What would it feel like to be a superhero in love?

In the 1980s, Alan Moore and Alan Davis considered this question in their groundbreaking reinterpretation of an obscure British hero named Marvelman—a character who had briefly flourished in the 1950s, as a shameless rip-off of the more famous American superhero, Captain Marvel. (In the US original, an ancient wizard grants young newsboy Billy Batson the ability to transform into a mighty superbeing on speaking the magic word, "Shazam!" In the British version, a mysterious astrophysicist grants young reporter Micky Moran the ability to transform into a mighty superbeing on speaking the magic word, "Kimota!"—that is, "atomic," spelled phonetically and backwards.) Like Captain Marvel, Marvelman possesses the standard superheroic gifts: great strength, apparent invulnerability, tremendous speed, and of course, the power of flight. But in Moore and Davies's revision, the gulf between the human and the superhuman was emblematized less by Marvelman's extraordinary physical abilities than by his capacity for love.

Consider, for example, this domestic scene. Mike Moran, no longer quite so young, talks with his wife Liz at the breakfast table. He complains that he feels alienated before his own super-heroic alter ego. "He's just so much *better* than I am," Moran admits. "At everything. His thoughts are like poetry or something. And . . . his emotions are so pure. When he loves you, it's gigantic. His love is so strong and direct and clean . . . When I love you it's all tangled up with who's not doing their share of the washing up, and twisted, neurotic little things like that."[1]

It's a short speech, but it combines profound aspiration with an acknowledgement of failure and a measure of self-conscious bathos— indicating among other things that the emotional dynamics of the superhero genre can be more nuanced than some critics acknowledge. It's also a confession of inadequacy that invites us to identify not with the icon of perfected masculinity who stands as the eponymous hero of the story, but with an altogether ordinary man. This man does not care much about bending steel with his bare hands or beating up bank robbers. He just wants to love his wife in a way that doesn't feel compromised by the banal character defects of his all-too-human nature—his acts of petty scorekeeping, his garden-variety narcissism. But, of course, he cannot always love her in that transcendent way, and the superhuman abilities of his heroic alter ego only exacerbate the point by exposing the painful limitations of his everyday incarnation. The irony is poignant, a reminder that even at our best we are rarely as good as we might wish to be. Little things like household chores get in the way of our finest feelings. Striving to grow spiritually, we get stuck on superficial trivialities that diminish our capacity for love.

At this moment, the superhero fantasy has become a self-reflexive allegory about the frustrations of human desire, with some obvious spiritual overtones. For it turns out that what Mike Moran really wants is to want his wife the way he does when he is Marvelman—which means what he really desires is a particular experience of desire itself. He wants to feel a love that is "like poetry," unsullied by either his own human imperfections or those of his no less human partner. He wants to feel a love that is gigantic, strong, pure, and that forgives all trespasses, great and small. In short, he wants to inhabit a structure of feeling that could best be described as divine. Indeed, this longing for an idealized experience of longing bears a more than passing resemblance to the divine etiology of desire that St Augustine famously traced, many centuries ago, when he argued that all sensations of earthly concupiscence were more or less distorted reflections of the soul's original and primary desire for God. Of course, the context is modern and secular, Moran's language is psychological rather than theological, and his choice of devotional object, in orthodox terms, is uxorious. But like Augustine, Mike Moran's awareness of the profound inadequacy of human love is grounded in his sense that more-than-human love is better.

For Alan Moore in *Marvelman*, then, to imagine loving like a superhero is to imagine loving like God—at least, according to several religious traditions. It is to imagine what it would be like to feel an infinite, compassionate, and forgiving love for even the lowliest and least deserving of creatures. But the actual effect of postulating this super-heroic variant on the experience of divine love turns out to be to focus our attention on the nature of human love and its limitations. This moment in *Marvelman* thus encapsulates a guiding assumption lying behind each of the chapters in this book: the idea that our fantasies of superhuman perfection can not only provide insight into our projections of the infinite, but also sharpen our conceptions of what it means to feel love, as finite and mortal beings, for others who are no less finite and mortal.

2

Having said this, I should swiftly add that I do not engage in arguments about the truth or falsehood of any particular religious doctrine in the course of the following pages. Nor do I propose to offer a series of allegorical readings of the superhero genre, "decoded" in the light of certain religious and mythical master-texts such as the New Testament, the Torah, or the works of Homer or Hesiod. Such analyses are plentiful enough, and I have learned from some of them; but this book does not really belong alongside them (for all that I sometimes find the temptations of allegory irresistible). Instead, to speak in the most general terms about my intentions, I have simply tried to approach superhero comics as fantastic, speculative, and distinctly modern expressions of a perhaps perennial human wish: the wish that things were otherwise.

Superhero comics address this wish in some of its most basic and fundamental manifestations. Who among us has not experienced frustration (at a minimum) over the limitations imposed upon us by our biological form? In superhero comics, there are no such limits: bodies perform impossible feats of strength, explode into flame, dissipate into vapor, flow like water, morph into animals, merge with machines, and perhaps most resonantly, defy the law of gravity, soaring effortlessly into the heavens.[2] Who among us can remain entirely sanguine in the face of the ultimate biological limitation of mortality? In superhero comics, death is rarely the end, and often seems more like an extended holiday, from which one eventually returns unharmed and perhaps even invigorated, with a new sense of purpose and a more stylish haircut and costume. Who has never felt anguish at the apparent gulf between our sense of what is just and the vagaries of fortune? Who has never felt anger at the way social and political "realities" contradict our sense of what is moral and right? In superhero comics—at least, during the first thirty years or so of the genre—the venomous, venal supervillains are always vanquished by the victorious forces of virtue![3] In fact, with their enhanced, elastic, and invulnerable-bodied characters, and the comfortingly schematic moral oppositions of their plots, superhero stories surely offer their readers some of the most primal fantasies of basic wish fulfillment available for commercial consumption: a veritable pornography of power.

Of course, for many commentators, this element of wish fulfillment is precisely the problem. It's all just too crudely, painfully obvious, and marks the entire genre as infantile and immature—something to be outgrown, at best. Speaking as an unabashed fan, I cannot deny that superhero comics often seem hyperbolic, even hysterical, in their denial of both our physical limitations and of the apparent moral indifference of the universe. But I also take very seriously the notion that such denials may actually be constitutive of the human. Here I follow the philosopher Susan Neiman, who has persuasively argued that the history of modern western thought can be productively understood in the light of our "refusal of the given as given—our capacity to make demands on reality."[4]

For Neiman, some of the most sophisticated intellectual work of the last three centuries has emerged from the tension or gulf between our sense of what *is* and our sense of the way things *ought* to be. In theological terms, this tension or gulf has traditionally been named "the problem of evil," and formulated in variants on the question of "How could a good God create a world full of innocent suffering?" But as Neiman points out, the problem of evil is "theological" in only the most narrow, historically circumscribed sense, because "nothing is easier than stating the problem of evil in nontheist terms. One can state it, for example, as an argument with Hegel: not only is the real not identical with the rational; they aren't even related." Elaborating on this point, Neiman continues:

> Every time we make the judgment *this ought not to have happened*, we are stepping onto a path that leads straight to the problem of evil. Note that it is as little a moral problem, strictly speaking, as it is a theological one. One can call it the point at which ethics and metaphysics, epistemology and aesthetics meet, collide, and throw up their hands. At issue are questions about what the structure of

the world must be like for us to think and act within it. . . .
I believe it [the problem of evil] is the place where philosophy
begins, and threatens to stop. For it involves questions more natural, urgent, and pervasive than the skeptical epistemological quan-
daries conventionally said to drive modern philosophy.[5]

If the superhero genre is an obvious fantasy-response to the distressing mismatch between our expectations of the world and the way the
world actually appears to be, then according to Neiman some of the
most influential figures in the history of modern thought—she dis-
cusses Rousseau, Hume, Kant, Sade, Hegel, and Nietzsche, among
others—have been crucially motivated by exactly the same distress.
Except "distress" turns out to be too mild a word for an intellectual
crisis so fundamental that it disrupts our conventional disciplinary
intellectual categories, forcing philosophers, theologians, and artists
alike to "throw up their hands" in confusion and despair.

Consequently, the very reason that some critics find superhero
comics contemptibly immature—the sheer *obviousness* of the refusal
to accept "the given as given" on display in these noisy, spectacular
and hyperbolic power fantasies—is also why I find them so wonderful: so entertaining, interesting, and profound. For although superhero comics are not commonly cited within our discussions of
theology, philosophy, or literature, to the extent that their appeal also
emerges from out of the gap between the *is* and the *ought*, between
the way things are and the way we'd like them to be, they engage with
some of the most fundamental questions that human beings know
how to ask.[6] As Neiman notes, "The fact that the world [apparently]
contains neither justice nor meaning threatens our ability to act in
the world and to understand it. The demand that the world be
intelligible is [therefore] a demand of practical and theoretical reason, the ground of thought that philosophy is called to provide."[7]
Superhero comics address themselves to this same threatening
meaninglessness—and to acknowledge this fact is to recognize that
"the demand that the world be intelligible" is no less a demand of
fantasy than it is of reason. Or rather, it is to recognize that fantasy
is *not* the opposite of reality, but is rather another way of making
sense of that reality. To this extent, fantasy has the same function as
reason, and cannot always be distinguished from it.[8] Indeed, the fact
that both reason and fantasy are "sense-making" processes helps to
explain why so many philosophers have reasoned themselves into

seemingly fantastic places, unable to say for sure whether they are awake or dreaming, or whether there are real causes of events rather than just the appearance of continuous conjunction. Even the keenest minds have sometimes had difficulty keeping the two processes—reasoning and fantasizing—apart.

To put the point still more provocatively: if the basic generic conventions of the superhero story—the miraculous powers and obsessive moral compulsiveness of their chief protagonists—attest to the strength of our demand that the world should make sense (and the depth of our fear that it may not), then perhaps those hyperbolic fantasies are not the absurdly unrealistic opposite of reasoned thought processes, but are rather vivid expressions of the normatively repressed anxiety, unreality, and even madness of reason itself. For if human endeavor really does take place in the context of an ultimately random, indifferent, and unintelligible universe, then reason is just another more or less crazy way of coping. After all, are Kant's obsessive ruminations on the categorical imperative really less insane than the idea of a man from another planet with godlike powers who always does the right thing? Is his suggestion that we should consider what would happen if our actions became universal laws of nature really that different from imagining what it would be like to have such godlike powers? And if not, is reading Kant's philosophy really any more likely to inspire moral action than simply asking the question, "What would Superman do?"

The purpose of these questions is not to denigrate the process of reasoned philosophical investigation into the nature of ethics (though I confess that I don't mind if I manage to annoy a few Kantians). On the contrary, I admire and value the work of philosophy to such a degree that I am actually trying to elevate the status of superhero comics by association. The point to be grasped, then, is that superhero comics draw much of their primary creative energy and appeal from the same rift between experience and desire that constitutes the beginning (and end) of modern philosophical inquiry—a space where traditional distinctions between philosophy, theology, and literature collide and break down—and that, unconstrained by the usual conventions of philosophical discourse, including the bar against overt acts of wish fulfilling fantasy, they can address some of the same profound questions. At the risk of provoking sneers from the skeptics I would therefore argue that superhero comics—brash, broad, and sometimes brutal melodramas though they are—often find themselves in the same conceptual territory as, say, *Also Sprach Zarathustra*, the *Bhagavad Gita*, and the tragedies of Shakespeare—texts that also happen to have a brash, broad, and sometimes brutal quality of melodrama about them, and that famously defy our traditional disciplinary categories by demanding to be read as philosophy, theology and literature, all at once. Therefore, I have attempted to read superhero comics in the way those more widely admired texts also demand to be read, shifting between the perspectives of the philosopher, the theologian, and the literary critic as and when it suits me—or, if you are willing to give me the benefit of the doubt, as and when it suits the material to be so addressed.

But why have I chosen these particular superhero comics to read? It could certainly be objected that I have not always selected "the best" examples of the genre for discussion in the following pages— nor even the most obvious ones, given my stated interests. Alan Moore's Dr. Manhattan in *Watchmen* probably represents the most ambitious attempt in the genre to date to imagine the superhero-as-divinity, but I have nothing to say about him; nor do I discuss the spiritual/kabalistic dimensions of Moore's more recent work in *Promethea*. And where's the extended analysis on the pantheist mysticism of Grant Morrison's most ambitious epics? Where's the close reading of apocalyptic Christian imagery in Mark Waid and Alex Ross's *Kingdom Come*? Where's the discussion of Manichean struggle and folkloric themes in Mike Mignola's *Hellboy*? Where's . . . well, you can insert your own favorite recent superhero text here.

It's certainly not my lack of interest or admiration for the work of these contemporary creators that has led me to overlook them here; in fact, I hope to find time to write about their comics one day, if only for my own benefit as a teacher. But for this project, I was more interested in looking behind the most obvious recent examples of the genre, to explore some historical texts at greater length than they are usually given in academic accounts. For that reason, the greater part of the superhero comics discussed here date from the so-called "Golden" and "Silver" ages—that is, from 1938 to the early 1970s.[9] With a couple of exceptions, then, these essays largely focus on comics and characters that were written and created before superheroes supposedly became "mature" in the 1980s—and one thing I hope they demonstrate is that just because something was regarded as "children's literature" at the time of its production, that does not mean that it is immature or simplistic; it does not mean that it is aesthetically crude; it does not mean that it cannot ask piercing questions; and it does not mean that so-called adults cannot learn from it. On the contrary, I think these older stories may sometimes do a better job than their more "adult" descendents when it comes to touching "the tender spots of universal human desires and aspirations, hidden customarily beneath long accumulated protective coverings of indirection and disguise," as William Marston so eloquently put it back in 1943.[10] In my opinion, the comics I have discussed here are "tales for all ages," in every sense of that phrase. And to the disappointed fans of the more contemporary superhero, I would add that many of the comics I read here are the same ones that Moore, Morrison, and the rest were reading as children. It was in *these* stories, and others from the first thirty or so years of the genre, that those later exponents of superheroic mysticism found their gods. Let's take a look at what they discovered.

3

The foregoing must stand as a broad defense of my particular academic interest in the superhero, if any such defense is required, and as a general description of my hermeneutic approach and choice of texts. But though the essays that follow blend diverse ideas and methodologies drawn from existential philosophy, psychoanalysis, feminist theology, cultural studies and formalist criticism, they are also united by their focus on that most earthly and spiritual of human experiences—love—the concept with which I began. To explain why this is so, I should perhaps say a little more about my use of that necessarily nebulous and sometimes disconcerting word, "spirituality," and its relationship to an over-lapping but non-identical concept of "religion."

I don't think that you have to believe in religion to believe in superheroes. But according to the deconstructionist theologian, John Caputo, in this current "post-secular" era, you don't actually have to believe in religion to believe in religion. You can have what he calls "religion without religion." What does that mean, exactly? Well, for Caputo, this paradoxical sounding possibility arises as a consequence of the secularizing drive of modernity, a drive that has ironically and unintentionally cleared the space for the return of a revitalized "post-metaphysical" religion. Caputo evokes Nietzsche as an unexpected prophet of the postmodern good news when he refers to what he also calls "the death of the death of God." He is nothing if not passionate in his views, which I will now quote at some length, in order to avoid distorting them, and also to give something of the sermonic flavor of Caputo's style:

> Marx and Freud always insisted (to the point of protesting too much) that they were scientific thinkers. But Nietzsche thought that science was just one more version of Christian Platonism, that the death of God implies the death of "absolute truth," including the absolutism of scientific truth.
>
> . . . Nietzsche's argument boomeranged in a way that nobody saw coming. What the contemporary post-Nietzschean lovers of God, religion, and religious faith took away from Nietzsche was that psychoanalysis (Freud), the unyielding laws of dialectical materialism (Marx), and the will to power itself (Nietzsche) are *also* perspectives, *also* constructions, or fictions of grammar. They are *also* just so many contingent ways of construing the world under contingent circumstances that eventually outlive their use-fulness when circumstances change. . . . Marx and Freud, along with Nietzsche himself find themselves hoisted with Nietzsche's petard, their critiques of religion having come undone under the gun of Nietzsche's critique of the possibility of making a critique that would cut to the quick—of God, nature, or history. Enlight-enment secularism, the objectivist reduction of religion to some-thing other than itself—say, to a distorted desire for one's mommy, or to a way to keep the ruling authorities in power—is one more story told by people with historically limited imaginations, with contingent concepts of reason and history, of economics and labor, of nature and human nature, of desire, sexuality, and women and of God, religion, and faith. . . . The declaration of the "death of God" is aimed at decapitating anything that dares Capitalize itself, which included not just the smoke and incense of the Christian mysteries but anything that claims to be the Final Word. That had the amazing effect of catching up hard ball reductionis-tic and atheistic critiques of religion in its sweep.
>
> . . . In this way of looking at things, the Enlightenment and its idea of Pure Reason are on the side of Aaron and the golden calf, while Nietzsche, God forbid, he who philosophizes with a ham-mer, stands on the side of Moses as a smasher of idols, and stands right beside Paul giving the Corinthians holy hell about the idols

of the philosophers. That opens the door for a notion like the love of God, the idea I love most of all, to get another hearing among the intellectuals. For it is a bald Enlightenment prejudice, unvarnished reductionism, to try to run that idea out of town and denounce it as sucking on your thumb and longing for mommy.[11]

Can I get an "Amen"? Well . . . maybe not. Caputo is an engaging writer, unafraid to take the risk of intelligibility in a realm filled with obscurantist charlatans, and his desire (expressed frequently elsewhere in his writings) to put the love of God back on a firmly social footing—making it a matter of "serving the poorest and most defenseless people in our society"—is entirely admirable. (Here, at least, Caputo's person-of-faith and Siegel and Shuster's original Superman really do have something in common, as my first chapter shows.) But what are we actually left with, if we "decapitate" all Capitalized concepts, as he suggests?

As Slavoj Žižek has pointed out, in a respectful but telling response to Caputo's work, we are left with "the well known post-modern meta-truth, the insight into the fact that there is no final Truth, that every truth is the effect of contingent discursive mechanisms and practices."[12] "God" thus becomes just another "name for radical openness, for the hope of change, for the always to come Otherness," and religion is "reduced to its pure destubstantialized form: a belief that our miserable reality is not all there is . . . that 'there is a another world possible,' a promise . . . of redemption-to-come betrayed by any ontological positivization." But in that case, as Žižek asks, why should anyone "go on praying?"[13] To put the point slightly differently, why does Caputo need the word "God"—let alone the more denominationally specific notion of Christianity— at all? If his faith finally boils down to a restatement of the idea that the wise man knows that he knows nothing, combined with the notion that we should all try and be nice to each other—and maybe redistribute some wealth while we are at it—then couldn't he find the support he needs in Socrates, Ms. Manners, and the *New Left Review*? Why steer us into the swampy territory of "religion" if we don't need to go there to end up at the place where Caputo has arrived?

Although he professes himself an atheist, Žižek is troubled at just how much Caputo appears to have given up in the course of taking his deconstructive theological turn:

In this "deconstructive" way, every . . . instantiation of the Divine is relativized . . . whenever we focus on a particular formulation . . . *ce n'est pa ça*. Within this space, there is simply no place for the paradox of Christian Incarnation: in Christ, this miserable individual, we see God himself, so that his death is the death of God himself. The properly Christian choice is the "leap of faith" by means of which we take the risk to fully engage in a singular instantiation of the Truth embodied, with no ironic distance, with no fingers crossed.[14]

In this essentially Kierkegaardian argument, the whole point of the Christian faith is the *necessity* of a total commitment to an absolute Truth, a commitment that mirrors the awesome character of God's own act of radical self-sacrifice for the sake of humanity, and that is therefore also a radical venture—a *risk*—a decision that might lead to suffering and even death. Being Christian, in this radically committed sense, is obviously difficult. George Herbert, perhaps the greatest Christian poet in the history of the English language, generated many lines out of the problem: "I have considered it," he wrote in one address to Christ, "and find, / There is no dealing with thy mighty passion."[15] The devotional bar is set very high, and most of us would probably not enjoy the company of anyone trying to reach it. But as Kierkegaard would no doubt respond, it's not a popularity contest. The point is, how deep is your faith? Just how far are you willing to go for the God you claim to believe in, the God that died for you? Are you also willing to die? Are you willing to kill? (Notoriously, Kierkegaard did not shy from this unnerving question. I consider his arguments in more detail in my third chapter on Spider-Man—a character whose commitment to the heroic role in the face of tremendous suffering closely resembles that of a Kierkegaardian "Knight of Faith.")

When contrasted with the passionate, radical, self-consciously anti-rational faith of a Kierkegaard, Caputo's religion-without-religion feels anything but risky. On the contrary, it starts to look like a cautious hedging of the metaphysical bet, a refusal to believe too strongly in anything at all on the grounds that we might incriminate ourselves, a kind of theological pledging of the Fifth Amendment. It might be the wiser position, the more reasonable position, and even perhaps the less harmful position. But would such an ontologically empty, "post-metaphysical" deity have inspired the actions of, say, a Dietrich Bonhoeffer, or an Etty Hillesum, or a Martin Luther King? Compared to those twentieth-century martyrs, Caputo seems a likeable, moderately liberal agnostic with a curiously sentimental attachment to the word "God"—a word he doesn't really need for his arguments about the importance of love, tolerance, openness, undecidability and all the other things he likes.[16] If this is postmodern religion, then I'm inclined to say give me that old-time kind. It's more courageous, and more honest, even if it's sometimes also (as Kierkegaard almost described Abraham) completely fucking insane.[17]

And there, of course, lies the problem. Because as Kierkegaard well understood, to display the kind of commitment to an idea—perhaps any idea—that Abraham displayed in his willingness to sacrifice Isaac is, precisely, insane. The choice between orthodox and postmodern religion thus seems to be a choice between a glorious, passionate, irrational, and—at the least—potentially self-destructive commitment on the one hand, and a safe, aseptic, bloodless detachment on the other. I know which perspective I admire more, but I also wouldn't blame anyone for not wanting to be tested in the way Bonhoeffer, Hillesum, and King were tested, and I would consider anyone who actively *desired* martyrdom crazy. Crazy with love, perhaps, but still crazy. And that madness can shade over into something much less admirable very quickly, if you decide that your idea of love is worth killing for as well as dying for. The line that separates a hero like Bonhoeffer from the kind of religiously motivated political assassin that we would repudiate in disgust is hardly self-declaring.

Thus it seems that on the one hand, we can embrace the passionate but potentially destructive madness of total commitment to a metaphysics of Truth, or, on the other hand, we can make a temporary selection from the vast array of lesser truths in the theological warehouse, like shoppers browsing an outlet mall. The range of "goods" can seem liberating, even intoxicating, until we realize that nothing will satisfy us for long—and that there is no way out of the mall and back to the church, because they knocked down the church in order to build the mall. Upon making this discovery, I find myself inclined to paraphrase Winston Churchill's famously self-canceling remark about democracy being the worst form of government: "postmodern religion is the worst form of religion, except for all those other forms that have been tried."

I have been round this altar a few times myself. When I was younger, I came up with my own version of the distinction between orthodox religion and Caputo's "religion without religion." I decided I wasn't religious, and didn't much like people who were, but that maybe I could be "spiritual." What I thought of as "religion"—genuflecting towards the two-thousand year old God of a bunch of desert patriarchs, or refusing to eat certain foods on certain days, or making everyone ashamed of their sexual desires, or just proclaiming that those who didn't see things your way were doomed for all of eternity—well, it seemed awfully cold and mean-spirited and unimaginative and just not a lot of fun. "Spirituality," on the other hand, was more appealing. It left open the possibilities of all kinds of groovy mysticism, and did not seem to require the condemnation of outgroups. What's more, far from being thorny and narrow, the "spiritual" pathways mapped by some of the late twentieth-century figures I most admired—the rock musicians of the 1960s, for example—seemed strewn with pleasures: art, music, poetry, sex, and drugs, for example. The sad truth, then, is that "spirituality" really appealed to me, not because it looked kinder or more tolerant than what I took to be "religion"—although it generally did seem that way—but because it looked easier and more enjoyable. Of course, Caputo doesn't intend his notion of "religion-without-religion" to signify in this teenage hedonistic way, but as an effort to make an end run around the horrors of dogma it too has the appeal of being more fun than the "old time" religion to which it is opposed—more intellectually sophisticated, and even cool and trendy in its invocations of all that wonderfully oracular theory and philosophy.

But nowadays, although I still adore The Beatles, and despise religious intolerance, I feel differently about just about everything else, and am embarrassed at the complacent ignorance of my former attitude. Without wishing to provide more details of my personal life than is absolutely necessary to make my point, I have come to realize that by a more substantial account, the notion of a "spiritual experience" involves a radical reorientation of values, and an unflinching inventory of the consequences of one's life and actions up to that moment. Although long familiar with artists and critics who spoke about "the temporary dissolution of the ego," I began to realize what that phrase actually meant, if taken seriously: a total loss of bearings, and a shattering of cherished illusions about the self, making certain old ideas and behaviors impossible to sustain, and leaving one raw, confused, and grieving. I also came to notice that in many spiritual texts—and perhaps in most of them—the first step on the path of genuine enlightenment is usually more of a hard shove.

I'm not saying that some kind of Pauline "Damascus moment" is a requirement for spiritual insight—just that it's common experience in many spiritual texts. I also believe that it is perfectly possible to rediscover your sense of joy, even after your world has been leveled by God's wrecking ball (though depending on the violence of the blow, it may not be easy, and it may take some time). I don't think that a spiritual outlook need be a tormented one, and certainly not any more so than a secular outlook. But what remains, after such an awakening, is a new awareness of the spiritual as marvelously simple in theory, and extraordinarily difficult in practice. Because the philosophies of figures like Christ, or the Buddha, or Mohammed, or Gandhi, are not terribly complex, in the end. Do unto others as you would have them do unto you. Don't be so selfish. Don't be so judgmental. Don't expect to get your way all the time. Try loving yourself as you are. Try love, period. This is not astrophysics or brain surgery. It's not Kant or Hegel or Lacan or Derrida or Jean-Luc Marion. It's more difficult than all of them. Be kind, you say? What . . . all day? Be kind *all day*?

The irony is that the religion I rejected, because I thought it looked difficult and restrictive, is actually a thousand times easier than this kind of spirituality. Saving yourself for marriage, not eating shellfish, covering or shaving or not shaving your head, hating infidels and burning heretics—by comparison, that stuff is *easy*. But loving your enemy? Loving your neighbor? Heck, loving yourself? Now, *that's* difficult—maybe as difficult as it gets.

As you will see, all the superheroes discussed in this book either teach this lesson, or discover it for themselves, the hard way. Thus, in what might turn out to be the biggest surprise for those readers who think of the superhero genre as predominantly about the pleasures of violent fantasy (in the unlikely event that any such readers have picked up this book), the real subject of all these essays turns out to be love. Superman teaches us just how miraculous it really is to be able to love one's enemy; Wonder Woman asks us to think about what it really means to surrender to love; Spider-Man discovers that love is the greatest risk that he can take; and Iron Man learns that unless he can admit his own need for love, and accept the vulnerability that goes along with it, his soul will die inside that shiny suit.

To conclude: it may be worth reiterating that my purpose here has not been to slip a proselytizing theological pamphlet into the pop culture section of the textbook store (as if to say, "hey kids, thinking about spirituality can be cool!"). Neither has it been my desire to prove that superheroes makes good grist for a variety of intellectual mills—although this is no doubt the case, and there's no shortage of books, ranging from the execrable to the enjoyable, that use the genre to explore such topics as education, philosophy, psychology, business, fashion, and physics, as well as religion. Unlike the authors of most of those books, however, I am at least as interested in making some claims for superhero comics themselves as I am in using them for illustrative purposes as part of some other project. I believe that the ethical and existential questions that inspire so many of our philosophical and theological inquiries are also *constitutive* of the superheroic fantasy. I believe that we hear and respond to the urgency and power of those questions when we are swept up in the experience of a superhero comic, in the same way that we hear and respond to the strains of gospel music in classic Rock & Roll—another popular, hybrid, and uniquely American art form that went global in the twentieth century—even if we do not even always consciously recognize the "spiritual" nature of the source. I further believe that superhero comics are especially, *generically*, suited to the task of engaging, expressing, and addressing urgent ethical and existential questions— and that it is partly because they can perform this task as well or better than some philosophers and churchmen that they have enjoyed such popular success.[18] I can offer no clinching proof for such an assertion, of course; but the essays that follow may serve as a kind of cumulative argument, as repeated demonstrations of the point.

In short, because this book is about superheroes, it cannot help but also be about spirituality—and consequently it is also about love. Finally, it is about how all three can kick your butt harder than any religion you have ever heard of. And I say we should thank the gods for that.

CHAPTER ONE

SUPERMAN: TRUTH, JUSTICE, AND ALL THAT STUFF

1

These days, everyone knows that Superman is really Jesus Christ—sent to Earth by his heavenly father to be raised as a mortal among mortals, perform miracles, and model the ultimate virtue of self-sacrifice. Except, of course, there are also those who know that Superman is not Jesus at all, but Moses—a savior-figure who escapes deadly peril as a baby in a floating capsule, to grow up gifted with great powers and burdened with great responsibilities. But then, there are those who see Superman as an obvious incarnation of the Egyptian god, Horus—the mightiest member of a race of other-worldly beings, deriving his magical abilities from the sun, and following a parental directive to protect the people in his charge. And then again, there are those who say that since Superman's stories resemble Greek myths more than those of ancient Egypt, he's really closer to Hercules—a colorful adventurer, half-god, half-mortal, best known for his serial feats of impossible strength.[1]

In fact, all these figures of religion and myth have been evoked at different times in discussions of Superman, and several more names could be added to this list. Their proliferation speaks to the pleasures and pitfalls of a kind of myth-criticism, heavily influenced by Joseph Campbell's venerable study, *The Hero With a Thousand Faces* (first published in 1949). The implications of Campbell's fascinating discovery that key elements of a heroic ur-narrative repeat themselves across different civilizations and time periods, sometimes independently—without evidence of cross-cultural influence—remain worthy of investigation and debate. As the basis of a critical strategy for the understanding of superheroes, however, claims that Superman is a costumed version of a Greek myth or a Galahad or a Golem often boil down to trite sounding observations in the "compare and contrast" mode, portentously proffered as evidence of a revealed mystery ("Superman is raised by surrogate parents; so is Moses!" "Superman is impossibly strong; so is Hercules!" "Superman wears a cape; Jesus doesn't!"). Many variations on this hermeneutic theme have been rung in the last few years, but the approach is ultimately limited.

One problem is that such arguments reveal more about the interpretive desire to claim Superman for this or that tradition (whether Jewish, Christian, or pagan) than they do about Superman himself. To that extent, they are idolatrous readings, in the precise sense articulated by philosopher-theologian Jean-Luc Marion, for whom "the idol acts as a mirror, not a portrait . . . [and then] masks the mirror because it fills the gaze."[2] Making an idol of Superman, and finding in him only an idealized reflection of our own preferred conceptual categories, we lose sight of his specific historical origins and transformations. Thus, critics who decode Superman in terms of a particular religion or myth invariably gloss over the fact that he is very much a product of popular modernism—first emerging during an era famously associated with the collapse of traditional belief systems and a widespread crisis of faith (not to mention the radical re-orientation of Western political ideology along the opposed axes of nationalistic democracy and totalitarianism).

To insist on Superman's origins in secular modernity is not to deny that his stories negotiate religious and mythical territory—of course they do. But so does T. S. Eliot's "The Wasteland," and the terms of *that* negotiation are notoriously complex. Rejecting the traditional critical prejudice against mass cultural forms, why should we assume that comic books are always simpler than poems when it comes to processing and transforming their primary materials?

Consequently, in this chapter, I do not propose to demonstrate that Superman is "really" a religious figure by performing yet another exegesis of his origin story (which I assume is familiar); nor do I attempt to claim him as a modern version of some ancient archetype by pointing out all the ways he resembles this or that character from heroic myth or folklore. For me, the enduring appeal and significance of Superman derives less from his resemblance to prior gods and heroes than from his status as one of the most successful modern mass-media attempts to depict what philosophers since Plato have called *the good*. Reading Superman's extended comic book history as a sustained pop-cultural effort to comprehend the nature of virtue, I do not mean to drain him of religious or mythic significance—far from it—but merely to indicate why he cannot be adequately explained by recourse to any single religious doctrine or mythic tale.

2

First, a confession: as a young comic book fan growing up in 1970s Britain, I didn't much care for Superman.

Don't get me wrong; I *wanted* to like him. Even as a preteen, I dimly recognized that he had a different kind of cultural clout from other comic book characters at that time. After all, he was a near ubiquitous pop culture figure, his image curiously equivalent to that of say, Elvis Presley, in that it was hard to remember a time before I had heard of him; it was as if Superman had always been there, as much part of my inherited universe as my own family. Moreover, his name might be dropped in grown-up conversations, in unexpected ways. Although I couldn't have put it in these terms at the time, looking back I recognize that he was already a potential touchstone in discussions of masculinity, US nationalism, and post-Nietzschean theology, which meant that he had a different kind of intellectual currency from his fellow comic book characters; he stood for things in a way that they could not. Other superheroes were registered trademarks, but only Superman was a philosophical concept. More accurately, he was a whole set of concepts.

Nevertheless, I thought Superman was *dull*.

For a start, he was simply too powerful. In the comics of the 1970s, there seemed no limit to his abilities, making it difficult for writers and artists to generate much in the way of dramatic tension. What's more, his powers defined the notion of bathos, running the gamut from the sublime to the ridiculous. Flight? Wonderful. Great strength and speed? Of course. Bulletproof skin? Sounds useful. X-ray vision? I can go with that. Heat vision? Telescopic vision? Microscopic vision? OK, you are starting to tread on even *my* threshold of disbelief. Super-breath? Now you're just being silly. What next? Super-farts? It was impossible for me to take a character with these kinds of abilities seriously.

But my problem wasn't simply that Superman was too physically powerful. He was also too well-adjusted psychologically. Prior to the "deconstruction of the super-hero" that some comics historians claim for the 1980s, Superman rarely doubted his mission or questioned his own motives and actions.[3] He never bickered with his super-friends, and the difference between him and the criminals he fought was always clear-cut. He may have been born on Krypton, but experientially he was a nice farm boy from Kansas. By contrast, Spider-Man was a self-obsessed teenage nebbish, the Fantastic Four were a dysfunctional family, the X-Men were social outcasts, and the Hulk was dangerously bad tempered and slow-witted. These characters had *real* problems. Superman only had fake ones. Sure, Lois thought Clark Kent was a loser-milquetoast, but the whole point was that she was wrong; he was just *pretending* to be a loser-milquetoast. The joke was always on her. Compared to Stan Lee's circus of fantastic but flawed crime-fighters, I thought that Superman was simply too good to be interesting.

Recently, however, I have come to realize that criticizing Superman for not conforming to conventions established at Marvel in the 1960s is a little like criticizing Louis Armstrong for not sounding more like The Beatles. Like all true originals, Superman cannot be fairly measured by comparison with his diverse imitators and would-be successors. Other superheroes can reveal what Superman *isn't*; but we have to shift our perspective in order to discover what he really is. And although I casually dismissed Superman for many years, I now think that the essence of his appeal, the core of his mythic significance, may depend upon the quality of unshakeable virtue that I once found so boring. In fact, viewed from a historical perspective, I think the attempt to characterize Superman in terms of essential goodness may constitute one of the more beautiful challenges that postindustrial popular culture ever produced for itself. (And I invoke the notion of beauty deliberately, by way of allusion to the convergence of aesthetics and ethics in our foundational philosophical texts.)[4]

On the way to describing this beautiful challenge, I will first raise the question of whether Superman has *any* genuinely essential qualities, in the strict sense of that term; it may be reductive to claim so much. After all, he has been around for more than 70 years now, not only as a mainstay of comics, but also as a successful figure in the history of radio, television, and film, and every different creative team in each of these different forms of media has given us a slightly different Man of Steel. I'm not talking about just minor stylistic choices (however telling those can be) but aspects of the mythology so indelibly part of our collective vision of Superman that it can be surprising to discover they were not there from the beginning.

Take those miraculous powers, for instance. As a young reader, I couldn't have known that it took almost 40 years for some of those abilities to develop. Indeed, few members of the general public probably realize that when Superman was first introduced in the 1930s, he couldn't even fly—and yet the power of flight is one of the first things that people associate with the character! He displayed that particular talent for the first time in the animated-cartoon features made by the Fleischer studio in the 1940s; but for at least the first year or so of his existence, he got around pretty well by means of prodigious leaping. Many of his other powers grew along similar lines. Denny O'Neil describes the process in an essay from the 1980s where, conveniently enough, he charts the development of super-breath. "In 1939, he could 'hold his breath for hours . . .'; in 1941, he blew out a raging fire; in 1947, he sucked back an escaping rocket; in 1959, he extinguished a star with one mighty puff."[5]

At the time of their introduction, each of these powers represented an exercise in creativity, as writers and artists attempted to surprise longtime fans, and perhaps also to outdo one another, with ever more unlikely displays of godlike ability. Superman's increasingly extraordinary stunts were thus part of the basic appeal of the Golden and Silver Age versions of the character. But by the more cynical 1970s, these miracles had become millstones around the necks of his continuity-bound creators. O'Neil's essay argues for a de-empowering of Superman, on the grounds that he had become too mighty to write; and since the mid 1980s, Superman's powers have been scaled back along the lines O'Neil suggested.

But if Superman's powers are not fixed, then what about other aspects of his legend? Again, for a person whose knowledge is confined to one dominant representation (the 1950s television series, say, or the Christopher Reeve movies) it can be surprising how piecemeal the origins of the mythology turn out to be. Of course, Jerry Siegel and Joe Shuster gave us a great deal in that epoch making first episode from the summer of 1938: the basic origin story (in just two panels!), the powers of strength, speed, and relative invulnerability ("nothing less than an exploding shell could penetrate his skin"), the Clark Kent identity, and a remarkable supporting character named Lois Lane. (In many ways, Lois is as much of an original as Superman at this early stage; independent and brave, but also ambitious and somewhat coldhearted, her cruel allure is sketched with masterly economy in her first appearance.) But it would be over a year later before we learned the name of his home planet and met Ma and Pa Kent for the first time, in an expanded version of the origin story; and the names of those adoptive parents proved particularly unstable, changing at different points from John and Mary to Eben and Sarah before settling on Jonathan and Martha. Superman's own Kryptonian name, Kal-El, was not revealed until 1942, in a prose novel by George Lowther entitled *The Adventures of Superman*. (Some critics have recognized Lowther's phrase as Hebraic in origin, and have translated it both as "swiftness of God" or as "all that God is.") Lowther was one of the chief writers of *The Superman Show*, a tremendously successful radio program in the 1940s; and it was through this radio program, not Siegel and Shuster's comic, that audiences first met *Superman's Pal, Jimmy Olsen*, and first learned of Superman's great weakness, Kryptonite (apparently introduced when the actor who played Superman insisted on taking a two-week vacation, as a means to cover his absence). The radio broadcasts also introduced an exchange of dialogue that still immediately evokes the character in the minds of millions: "Look! Up in the sky! It's a bird! It's a plane! No, it's . . . Superman!"

Superman's enemies have also changed since those early days. One of the most remarkable things about Siegel and Shuster's first year of stories is the absence of superpowered villains. Instead, as might befit the creation of two idealistic Jewish-American men from depression-era Cleveland, Superman fought the representatives of a greedy, corrupt social elite. Over the course of his first 12 appearances he brings down a greedy senator with ties to arms manufactures; punishes a mine owner for forcing his men to work in dangerous conditions; exposes a disingenuous advertising executive out to fleece the public; and attacks dishonest stockbrokers in the oil industry. (He also addresses problems such as ghetto housing—which he explicitly declares a causal factor in youth crime—campaigns for prison reform, investigates the relationship between poverty and gambling, and takes on corruption in the sporting world!)[6]

Let's reflect for a moment on the idea of virtue represented by this original Superman. Writer Jerry Siegel had not yet found a snappy slogan to summarize the moral imperatives driving his new hero, and so the language with which he introduces the character varies slightly from issue to issue, but the concept of the "battle against oppression" quickly emerges as a constant. Siegel's Superman is "a champion of the oppressed" (*Action Comics* #1); "dedicated to assisting the helpless and oppressed" (*Action Comics* #6); "[engaged in a] one-man-war against the forces of evil and oppression" (*Action Comics* #8); and even a "savior of the helpless and oppressed" (*Action Comics* #9). In other words, the good that Superman does is explicitly characterized from the outset as a form of sociopolitical intervention. In a world where some have power and some do not, the virtuous man—Superman—is on the side of the have-nots. The relationship between virtue and politics is rendered even more explicit in the stories themselves, for the "evils" that most exercise the character are clearly rooted in economic inequality. "Justice," for Siegel and Shuster's original Superman, is less a matter of individual rights than a matter of the distribution of wealth.

Finally, and most radically, this Superman not only asserts the primacy of a moral economy over and above that of the market economy, but he does so without regard for the laws of his society protecting the sanctity of property. This violation of property law is most vividly apparent in a story from *Action Comics* #12 (cover date, May 1939). Like most of these early Superman strips, this one was originally untitled, although it is listed on the contents page of the 2006 reprint anthology, *Superman Chronicles: Volume One,* as "Superman Declares War on Reckless Drivers." This contemporary heading is slightly misleading, however, for over the 13 pages of this classic tale Superman does not confine himself to chasing down individual motorists. He also destroys cars that have been impounded by the police for traffic infractions (deeming the mere confiscation of the vehicles insufficient punishment), wrecks the inventory of a car salesman on the grounds that the vehicles are unsafe, and, finally, assaults an automobile factory. Before Superman "gleefully runs amuck" destroying the place, he pauses to explain his actions to the factory owner: "It's because you use inferior metals and parts so as to make higher profits at the cost of human lives!" (see Figure 1.1).

Figure 1.1 In *Action Comics* #12 (1939) Jerry Siegel and Joe Shuster's socialist-anarchist Superman literally attacked the capitalist system. © DC Comics.

Ralph Nader fans, take note—Superman here anticipates the basic argument of *Unsafe at Any Speed* by a quarter century, offering an explicitly economic analysis in which the ideology of capitalism bears at least as much responsibility for deadly road accidents as the individual driver. More than a vociferous consumer advocate, however, Superman then directs his anger at the system by destroying private property, directly halting the means of production. That these acts are violations of the law is underlined in more than one panel, wherein blue-uniformed policemen ineffectually attempt to prevent his destructive rampage. Given that we are still intended to see Superman as a virtuous figure, the moral message is explicitly revolutionary. The social order is represented as corrupt to the extent that true moral action cannot inhere in its laws and practices. The virtuous man must therefore break the law.

Like more than one great political philosopher, however, Jerry Siegel hedges on the crucial matter of whether Superman's virtuous revolutionary action is directed towards the attainment of a single "common good" that will ultimately benefit every member of society, or whether he thinks different social groups will always be divided by irreconcilable notions of the good.[7] If the latter situation obtains, then all would-be moral agents must pick a side—which would seem to place Superman squarely in opposition to the ruling democratic-capitalist institutions of the day. However, the story climaxes with Superman forcing the mayor of the city (not yet named Metropolis) to confront the consequences of his failure to enforce safety regulations by kidnapping him and dragging him to see the remains of road accident victims at the morgue. In light of this experience the horrified bureaucrat has an epiphany: "You've shown me this from a viewpoint I never saw before! I swear I'll do all in my power to see that traffic laws are rigidly enforced by the police!" The implication, of course, is that the legal system was not entirely at fault, but merely inadequately prosecuted—with the further suggestion that our leaders can be counted on to do the right thing once shown the error of their ways.

But this optimistic denouement can hardly contain the radicalism of a vision in which Superman "gleefully" destroys private property and terrorizes an elected official, all in the name of a higher good. The creative energy of the story clearly derives from the thrill of depicting his simultaneously anarchic and yet highly moralized assault upon the intertwined evils of rampant corporatism and inadequate governmental oversight. Moreover, one can hardly blame Siegel for hedging. In the absence of his final, less-than-convincing gesture toward the possibility of a rapprochement between his hero and the political apparatus of capitalist democracy, we would seem to have been proffered an explicitly Marxist vision of ethics—and even in the late 1930s, such statements were unusual in the popular culture of the United States, and carried a significant risk of backlash. It was probably only the official status of comic books as a relatively new form of children's literature that allowed Siegel and Shuster to get away with as much as they did during this first year. For in the early days of their existence, comic books generally flew below the radar, as too insignificant for the nation's cultural gatekeepers to notice. As sales climbed, and the comic book business was transformed from a vestigial wing of commercial publishing into a massively popular and lucrative form of entertainment, this situation would change.

4

So how was this fabulously subversive socialist Superman displaced and then erased from cultural memory? Well, it didn't take long before the comic book industry—an industry that grew up largely on the back of Superman's unprecedented early success—started to draw the fire of social conservatives.[8] As early as May 1940, Sterling North, literary editor of the *Chicago Daily News*, initiated the first "anti-comic book" campaign in the country, and in the words of comics historian Gerard Jones, "what he said struck a deep chord. Confronted . . . with an alien entertainment form that had come from nowhere to infiltrate the taste of seemingly every child in America, adults reacted with a collective gasp."[9] North's campaign never reached the fever pitch of the more famous crusade of Dr. Fredric Wertham a few years later; but Jack Leibowitz, co-owner of National Allied Publications (later DC Comics), read the writing on the wall and moved quickly to protect his properties. He hit upon a plan to insulate Superman, Batman, and the other DC heroes from criticism by establishing them as entirely wholesome creations, in accordance with the normative, mainstream standards of the era. Among other measures, he created new editorial policies dictating that DC's heroes did not kill, and prohibited further stories depicting the destruction of private property, except by obvious villains.

Siegel and Shuster chafed at some of these restrictions—for instance, Leibowitz's insistence that they maintain silence on the subject of Nazism (a position he only relaxed after Pearl Harbor, when popular opinion turned against isolationism).[10] But ultimately, they too were seduced by the inevitable temptations that came in the wake of Superman's unanticipated and unprecedented success. Although the decision to take Superman in a less radical direction was initially impelled by the forces of conservative reaction, the analysis of visual media scholar Ian Gordon rings true: "Superman's social activism dissipated as his owners and creators grew aware of his potential as a commodity."[11]

The project of re-inventing Superman according to less revolutionary ethical standards was therefore already well underway when the United States finally entered World War II in 1941, but the circumstances of that conflict accelerated and shaped the process. Comic book sales doubled during the war years and researchers have attributed much of that growth to American servicemen, with almost 60 percent of the population of military training camps during the period copping to the comic book habit.[12] Superman and Batman themselves were kept out of the European theater, in part because Superman was already too powerful to be placed in "real" combat settings; but as Gordon notes, DC successfully "aligned the characters with home front campaigns for responsible consumption—an alignment that led to Superman's identification with the American way."[13] When Siegel and Shuster lost a legal battle with DC over ownership of the character in 1948 and were replaced by new writers and artists, the transformation of the character from the political fringe to the mainstream could be taken as complete. With the names of his creators removed from the byline, the last traces of the original Superman had been wiped away.

By the 1950s, Superman's ideological leanings were entirely in step with those of the political establishment. Partly as a result of his wartime "service," Superman came to symbolize an ideological system in which America was regarded as the "leader of the free world," both militarily and morally.[14] In the highly popular television series of that decade, Superman was given a new slogan. He now stood for "Truth, Justice, and the American Way"—and however one defines those nebulous concepts, the point to be grasped is that during this period they were not only proffered as synonymous but also effectively encapsulated by the image of a happily assimilated superpowered alien, dressed in a red-and-blue body stocking. Superman had become one of America's self-chosen idols: a spectacular figure who both captured and flattered the gaze of the nation with an idealized vision of itself.

However, as the political landscape within and beyond the borders of the United States changed over the ensuing decades, Superman's association with the hegemonic conservatism of 1950s America harmed him more than Kryptonite ever could. During the 1960s, his adventures came to seem remote from the conflicts and concerns uppermost in the minds of the baby boomers, such as the war in Vietnam, the rise of feminism, and the problem of racism. Naïve and dreamlike, the best Superman stories of the era have an almost Dadaist charm, with their frequent reliance on surreal time-travel and parallel universe stories, and the introduction of the absurd but loveable characters of Krypto the Superdog and Bizarro the reverse-Superman. But by the end of that tumultuous decade, Superman comics could easily seem childish next to the hipper and more politically engaged Marvel titles of the day. After all, Stan Lee's *The Amazing Spider-Man* took place in a world where racial tension, environmental pollution, prison riots, civil disobedience, rock music, and drugs were all part of the fabric of the hero's experience. By comparison, Superman was not so much floating above it all as on another planet—often literally. He was still identifiable as a nice guy, but about as clueless as Dylan's Mr. Jones.

Small wonder, then, that by the 1970s, cultural critics began to condemn Superman as an establishment figure. Umberto Eco went so far as to declare that the character represented "a perfect example of civic consciousness completely split off from political consciousness." Noting Superman's tendency to punish bank robbers in between "benefit performances . . . for orphans and indigents" Eco wonders, somewhat condescendingly, why Superman does not "liberate 600 million Chinese from the yoke of Mao?" (It doesn't occur to him that this is a little like asking why movie Nazis speak English in bad "Cherr-man ack-zents" rather than their native language. The answer is that all genre fictions rest on conventions that must simply be accepted by their audiences if they are to be enjoyed. It can be interesting to note the form these conventions take; but criticizing Superman for his failure to liberate the Chinese is on par with pointing out that Philip Marlowe's career as a private eye is incompatible with his personal integrity, or asking why Dr. Who does not use his advanced alien technology to provide contemporary humans with a cure for cancer—or why the Batmobile never gets stuck in traffic.)

Eco concludes that Superman's notions of good and evil are woefully limited: "As evil assumes only the form of an offense to private property, good is represented only as charity."[15] Eco's essay is something of a touchstone in academic discussions of the Man of Steel and is generally cited approvingly, despite his apparent ignorance of the character's progressive origins. For example, Patrick L. Eagan acknowledges and elaborates on Eco's argument when he declares that, in Superman's world "the essential function of government is . . . rooted in the necessity to control human behavior that is selfish or ignorant . . . to save us from ourselves. This is the very role, of course, that Superman aspires to . . . fans . . . will find few, if any, examples of their hero exercising his powers to bring about the real and lasting improvement of the human condition; rather they will find . . . an obsession with preserving the status quo."[16] By the 1980s, it wasn't just the critics who regarded Superman's conception of "the good" with suspicion. Other members of the superhero community seemed to see him as a boy scout at best, and as an all-too-willing dupe of authority at worst. Perhaps most notoriously, in Frank Miller's *The Dark Knight Returns*, Batman condemns his former super-friend as a government toady before handing him the worst beating of his life.[17]

The presumption of moral superiority that underwrote the political ideology of 1950s America now appears laughable, and to the degree that Superman may once have emblematized such notions he is obviously vulnerable to the various charges of ethical retardation, status-quo-ism, and toadyism that have been laid at his scarlet-booted feet. However, after reading the actual comics—the best of them, at least—these critiques can start to seem a little misplaced, if not unfair. As I've already suggested, many Superman stories of the 1950s and 1960s read more like surreal sci-fi fairy tales than propaganda for the capitalist principle of property rights. Often their subtextual themes seem more psychological than political—as in the explorations of Superman's Kryptonian origins, for example, that are readily interpretable as allegories of loss.[18] Many other stories of the 1960s are self-described as "imaginary" (a curious near-tautology in the context of the genre), and are intended to be enjoyed as "thought experiments" without long-term implications for the continuity of the series. In other words, Superman's comics in the 1960s were often speculative, self-reflexive, and strangely self-canceling— framed by editorial reminders that "this didn't actually happen." All this is hardly what one would expect from Eco or Eagen's characterization of Superman as the ultimate defender of the contemporary capitalist order.

Moreover, during the 1970s and 1980s, Eco's criticisms were sometimes explicitly anticipated and addressed within the pages of the comics themselves. Consider, for example, a famous and frequently reprinted story first published the same year as Eco's essay, in *Superman* #247 (January 1972), written by Elliot Maggin and entitled "Must There Be a Superman?" In this tale, the Guardians of the Universe—an advanced alien race—confront Superman with the idea that his presence on Earth may actually be inhibiting the moral development of ordinary humanity. Later, when Superman intervenes to prevent a young Mexican immigrant from being beaten by an American farmer, he encounters (as if for the first time) a larger system of economic exploitation that shocks him into paralyzed self-questioning. He agonizes over the question of how his powers might be used in a way that would actually help an impoverished community of migrant farm workers, and eventually concludes that while he can directly assist them in the face of natural disasters—rebuilding their homes after an earthquake, for instance—he can only encourage a labor strike from the sidelines. Thus, in the final pages of the story he tells them "you must not count on a Superman. . . . Young Manuel . . . has the right idea! When the rest of you backed down [to the bosses], Manuel refused to knuckle under. . . . You don't need a Superman! What you really need is a Super-Will to be guardians of your own destiny."

Of course, this resolution hardly seems satisfactory, but as the Guardians of the Universe tell us at the close of the story, that's almost the point. Their mission was to leave the Man of Steel (and, by extension, the reader) "troubled." And while it would be easy enough to complain that Superman falls back upon a classically conservative argument about the potentiality of the autonomous individual will as his excuse for doing nothing, we should also note that Maggin has smuggled a sophisticated and perhaps even irresolvable ethical problem into a supposedly naïve heroic mythos. Forced to consider not just a single "real world" instance of racial and economic injustice, but also the complex social and national histories in which that injustice is embedded, Superman is undone by his recognition of a painful truth. Even when combined with a sincere will to do the right thing, tremendous power does not necessarily translate into virtuous action, because it is not always clear what the virtuous action might be in any given situation. In some political situations a "purely" virtuous act—if normatively defined as an act that injures no one—may be impossible. In a further twist, the story even hints that Superman's scrupulous desire to do good is itself as part of the problem. For while his decision to respond to the plight of exploited migrant farm workers with a cheerleading speech may seem inadequate, it is presented as a sincere effort to strike a balance between charitable action and paternalistic intervention—that is, between providing genuinely helpful assistance and imposing his will in a potentially authoritarian and infantilizing way. If Superman does the wrong thing, it would seem to be for the right reasons. To put it another way, if Superman fails here, then so do we all. After all, the frequent disparity between our moral intent and the results of our actions remains a sticking point within every ethical system yet devised; and no human society has yet managed to resolve or transcend the structures of inequality and exploitation that are the real evils of this story.

5

In sum, between the late 1930s and the early 1970s, Superman's virtue manifests itself in a series of different ways, within a series of different ideological formations that alter almost by the decade, and in accordance with broader historical contexts: from thinly veiled revolutionary socialism to wartime populism to Eisenhower capitalism to self-canceling escapism to inhibiting self-skepticism. Thus, Superman's history illustrates a simple but powerful idea that has rendered problematic every attempt to found a universalist ethics or transcendentalist theory of justice, from Plato to Kant to Rawls: good and evil are not absolutes, but change according to time, place, and culture.[19] As the foregoing pages show, they can change profoundly and with remarkable rapidity even within the same culture.

The point I want to emphasize, however, is not that virtuous action is something of a moving target, but that Superman apparently must move with it. Whatever we collectively imagine "good" to be at any given time, it seems that Superman must strive to be that, too. And this observation, finally, brings me to the beautiful and challenging idea I mentioned several pages ago as constitutive of the Man of Steel. For what Superman's transformations reveal, beyond the historical contingency of moral value, is the commitment of the character to the ideal of moral perfection. Superman imaginatively defies the very contingency of value that his publication history embodies—and moreover, he requires the same imaginative defiance from us. Our ethical conceptions may be partial, contingent, and limited, and we can expect those limitations to be exposed with hindsight or in unforeseen situations; but nevertheless, even in the face of this familiar moral *aporia*, the beautiful challenge that Superman sets for his creators—and for his audience—is the challenge of imagining what an absolute commitment to virtue might look like, if only it were possible. It may therefore be no exaggeration to say that, while the form and register are obviously different, Superman's beautiful challenge to his creators and readers is ultimately the same challenge faced by all serious ethical philosophers since Aristotle.

While scenes of thrilling action and displays of tremendous physical power are obviously necessary components of any Superman story, they are less important than his ability to project convincing moral authority. Just how important this ability is to the character was made clear in his most recent cinematic adventure, *Superman Returns* (2006). In a tiny but crucial scene that signifies on multiple levels, the editor-in-chief of the Daily Planet, Perry White (played by Frank Langella), instructs his crew of reporters on how to cover the story of Superman's return to Metropolis after an absence of some years. "Does he still stand for Truth?" Perry asks. "For Justice?" A pause. "All that stuff."

Truth, Justice, . . . and all that stuff? Don't let the disingenuously casual idiom fool you. Tectonic shifts in the continental plates of ideological fantasy and ethical awareness are implied by such tiny acts of cultural re-encryption, and if we listen carefully we can hear the reverberations resounding. At the heart of this American film about a quintessentially American icon, we can detect a loss of confidence in the moral validity of "The American Way" itself. Perry White's generic and generalizing phrase ("all that stuff") is revealingly poignant: an obvious evasion that in its very circumlocution exposes an obscure embarrassment, a barely acknowledged shame. Because we know—we *all* know—what the phrase "all that stuff" occludes. We know what we used to say, and what it seems we can no longer bear to say. And even if we no longer know exactly what "The American Way" stands for, we clearly know what it *doesn't* stand for, what it cannot even pretend to stand for, in the early years of the twenty-first century. It doesn't stand for "Truth and Justice." After the lies that led to the invasion of Iraq, after the policies of extraordinary rendition, after the sanctioning of torture at home and abroad, after the no-bid contracts to Halliburton, KBR, and Blackwater— after all these and many other well-documented examples of the appalling abuse of power by the Bush administration—well, even Superman couldn't bring the concepts of "Truth, Justice, and The American Way" together anymore.

But even when America itself can no longer persuasively evoke moral authority, Superman must try. Constantly striving toward but never reaching the ever-receding horizon of absolute virtue, Superman has become a rare and paradoxical artistic creation at such a moment: a fiction that remains true to itself only by being severed from its point of origin; a representation of the good whose entire career suggests that the good can only be gestured toward, but never represented; and a figure that stands, with precise imprecision, for "Truth, Justice . . . and all that stuff."

6

In conclusion: taking a historicized view of Superman's comic book adventures since 1938 we can see them as a series of attempts to represent a moral agent who acts always out of his commitment to "the good"—a good that for the purposes of the narrative is conceived as absolute, but that is also never more than loosely defined. Because this notion of the "good" is constantly shifting and only ever partially descried, it will always be reductive to try to explicate Superman in terms of a single belief system such as Judaism or Christianity, or in terms of a prior mythic tradition. In this respect, we can say that the "spirituality" of Superman is nondenominational. However, we are still in the presence of a kind of spirituality, in an important formal sense; for to the extent that Superman is defined by an absolute and *a priori* commitment to a finally unverifiable and unknowable good, he reproduces in himself the formal structure of all acts of religious faith. Thus, we might say, Superman's ethics are theological in form while remaining indeterminate at the level of content.

I have also suggested, perhaps somewhat counterintuitively, that Superman's moral beauty is more essential to his character—and perhaps in some sense more extraordinary—than his spectacular powers. This fact may not always have been apparent, even to his creators, in his earliest years; but for each successive generation of writers and artists, steeped in Superman's complex history, and anxious to add a "classic" story to the Superman canon, the nature of Superman's ethical purity has become a more central concern. As stories like Maggin's "Must There Be a Superman" make clear, as long ago as 1972, Superman's creators were not content with a hero whose idea of the good was limited to acts of charity and the protection of property. In the decades since, many stories have appeared that portray his commitment to the good not in terms of politics or the law but as a kind of devotion—in both the religious and amorous senses of that word. Indeed, in his relationships with his supporting cast, Superman nowadays manifests a selflessness that borders on the excessive.[20] The excessive (and hence "religious") quality of this devotion emerges most clearly not in his interactions with lovers and friends like Lois and Jimmy, but in his relationship with his greatest foe, Lex Luthor.

When I was a younger reader, Luthor was yet another aspect of the Superman myth that I just didn't get. How could it be that Superman's greatest foe had no superpowers of his own? How could a B-movie "mad scientist" present a serious threat to a creature capable of blowing out the stars like birthday candles on a vast, cosmic cake? But now I recognize that Luthor's limitations are precisely the point. He is, in the most literal sense, Superman's best foil: the element in the design that allows us to see the inner light of the jewel.

The fact that Luthor has no superpowers, but is nevertheless driven by an overwhelming need to be dominant, helps us to recognize the absence of any will-to-power in Superman himself.[21]

To put the argument in slightly different (but no less Nietzschean) terms, if Superman is more than human then Luthor is all too human. Even the greatest thing about him—his all-consuming hatred for Superman—is undermined by the sheer banality of its etiology. In the 1960s version of his origin (a late story by original creator Jerry Siegel), Luthor's enmity towards the Man of Steel was said to stretch back to an incident when both characters were teenage boys in Smallville; Superboy saves Luthor from a laboratory fire, but in the process Luthor is exposed to a chemical spill that causes his hair to fall out.[22] On the one hand, this may seem petty fuel for a lifelong vendetta, even for a comic book villain. But on the other hand, it is a remarkably vivid emblem for the way narcissistic injuries can generate resentments. What's more, at least since the tale of Samson and Delilah, the shearing of a man's hair has signaled emasculation. Luthor's baldness, then, may symbolize not only his status as an "evil egghead," but also his wounded masculine ego—a surface marker indicating the depth of his disavowed feelings of inferiority. In Luthor's later incarnations the Smallville lab accident is some- times written out, but the emotional subtext of the story, with its suggestion that Luthor's hatred for Superman is rooted in feelings of adolescent envy, inferiority, and wounded narcissism, remains the same.

Luthor thus reminds us that while the consequences of evil may be spectacular, its origins are often ordinary: egotism, fear, jealousy, greed. These everyday feelings, finally, are the chief province of this least "super" of all super-villains, and they are also familiar to all of us. If we cannot identify a little with Luthor, then I think we cannot hope to see what is so interesting about his enemy.

In other words, Luthor is Superman's arch-nemesis *because* of his human weaknesses and not in spite of them. It is Luthor's job to remind us how hard it is for human beings to be genuinely good, and how ordinary and banal the origins of human evil really are. But Luthor also makes it possible for us to recognize one more miracu- lous—and beautiful—aspect of his chosen nemesis. For despite all Luthor's machinations, all his destructive acts, and all his petty motivations, Superman never returns his hatred. Luthor can make him wrathful, but never hateful—and in one of the better Superman stories of recent years, he responds to Luthor's murderous egotism with extraordinary sensitivity, tolerance, and even kindness.

The comic I have in mind is Grant Morrison and Frank Quitely's *All Star Superman* #5, entitled "The Gospel According to Lex Luthor." Most of the action takes place in a high security prison, where Luthor has been sentenced to death row for his various crimes. Superman, in the guise of Clark Kent, arrives to interview Luthor for his newspaper. Luthor pompously insists upon his high motives while simultaneously revealing his deep prejudices—"Imagine life on this world if some opportunistic alien vermin hadn't decided to dump it's trash here," he says at one point—but most of all, the impression he gives is of absurd vanity. Not only bald, but also lacking eyebrows, he paints on the missing features with make-up. He is also completely out of touch with the reality around him; as he and Kent walk around a supposedly secure wing of the prison, talking, a series of disasters occur—the super-villain The Parasite temporarily escapes, a riot breaks out—but Luthor simply proceeds, obliviously secure in his own power and authority. On several occasions he is almost killed; Superman, as Kent, saves him every time, usually in the guise of clumsiness (knocking Luthor out of the path of a bullet, for example). Luthor fails to notice and is without gratitude.

The only time in the story that Luthor expresses something close to vulnerability is when he realizes that one of his painted eyebrows has been smeared off during the confused events of the day. Turning away in embarrassment and reaching for his eyebrow pencil he coughs and mutters, "What are you looking at Kent?" But Kent/Superman feigns not to notice; he is cleaning his glasses, and claims that he cannot see anything without them. (Morrison's insistent self-referentiality can sometimes be distracting, but here the use of Kent's famously inadequate "disguise" to reveal Superman's essential kindness is nicely subtle.)

At such poignant moments, we see that only Luthor's vanity could allow him to think of Superman as his enemy. In fact, Superman is his gentle savior—so gentle that even as he preserves Luthor's life, Superman allows him to maintain his illusions of power and control. Thus, through Luthor, we see that Superman's devotion to humanity is such that even the worst of us will always be treated with infinite patience and compassion. The results are both funny and moving, and leave the reader in no doubt as to the most incredible aspect of

Superman's character. Few human beings are ever so good. This, perhaps, is the final, paradoxical lesson that we can draw from the 70 years and more of Superman's adventures—that it may be easier to fly, to see through walls, and to outrace a speeding bullet, than it is to love your enemy.

CHAPTER TWO

WONDER WOMAN: BONDAGE AND LIBERATION

1

In the 1940s, during the commercial heyday of the comic book industry, Wonder Woman was one of the most successful superheroes in the business. Appearing in three different monthly comics with combined sales in the millions, for a time she was even bigger than Superman. Later, in the 1970s, she achieved good ratings as the star of a hit TV series, and was celebrated as an icon of women's liberation by no less an authority than Gloria Steinem (who put her on the cover of *Ms.* magazine). But in more recent decades, her fortunes have fallen. Her comic book sales have sometimes dipped perilously close to cancellation levels; and while other superheroes have enjoyed great success at the box office over the last few years, Wonder Woman seems permanently trapped in preproduction purgatory. Adding insult to injury, Hollywood starlet Megan Fox dismissed the character as "lame" when asked if she would consider playing the part.[1] Seemingly unaware of Wonder Woman's historic association with the struggle for women's rights, Fox expressed pity for any actress who took the role. Numerous Internet commentators echoed her skepticism. Nowadays, it seems, Wonder Woman gets no respect.

Several factors have contributed to this drop in Wonder Woman's pop-cultural stock, not least the memory of that 1970s TV show; while gloriously kitschy, it led many audience members to regard the concept as inherently less "serious" than that of, say, Superman or Batman (although the obvious contrast between the similarly kitschy Batman TV show of the 1960s and the grim portrayal of the Caped Crusader in his most recent movies should give the lie to that assumption). The historical specificity of Wonder Woman's World War II origin also adapts less straightforwardly to modern media retellings than the story of either of her Golden Age rivals. And good old-fashioned sexism has played its part, too; depressingly, it might have been easier to persuade a predominantly male comic book audience to follow the adventures of a female superhero in the cultural milieu of the 1940s than it is today.[2]

But Wonder Woman has always presented some special difficulties to her creators. Contradictions abound. As Marc Edward DiPaolo has observed, in a wide-ranging essay on the character, Wonder Woman is a "warrior pacifist, a feminist sex symbol, a foreign-royal-turned-American-immigrant, and a devout pagan living in a secular age."[3] I'd add a few more items to this list of ironies. For example, although conceived and at least for a time widely perceived as inspirational to women, the great majority of Wonder Woman's comic book adventures have been written and illustrated by men. Then there's the intriguing fact that, while locked for decades in a (mostly) unrequited love affair with the (mostly) unworthy Steve Trevor, she has nevertheless been vilified—and embraced—as a figure of lesbian desire and queer identification.[4] Consequently, it's hardly a surprise that sometimes even her publishers seem uncertain as to her target audience. Does she appeal more to girls, or boys? To girls *and* boys? To gay boys and straight girls or gay girls and straight boys? (The answer is apparently all of them, sometimes, and not enough of any of them, now.)

I believe that these contradictions and confusions arise from the essentially deconstructive impulse that impelled her original creation—and here I use the term "deconstruction" in its most precise sense. A basic premise of deconstructive theory is that the discourses of Western thought—and particularly the vocabularies of philosophy, theology, and literary criticism—have been shaped, or haunted, by a series of powerful binarisms. If the governing binary is that of God/human, then descending from it in parallel structure we can include the antagonistic couplings of: man/woman, spirituality/sexuality, mind/body, master/slave, reason/emotion, truth/rhetoric, and science/art. A reader trained in the interpretive strategies of deconstruction would not only note the hierarchical nature of these oppositions when they are invoked, but also attempt to invert these hierarchies by exposing the repressed dialectical interdependence of the paired terms—demonstrating through close reading that these supposed dichotomies are actually mutually defining concepts, each needing the other to make sense, although this mutual implication is generally glossed over for rhetorical purposes.[5]

The characteristically double insight of this branch of textual analysis is therefore: first, that binary oppositions have enormous explanatory, sense-making force (indeed, to the extent that all abstract thought requires us to bundle the impossibly rich profusion of experience into manageably reduced categories of "this" or "that," it may not be possible to think entirely outside of them); and second, that binary oppositions nevertheless serve simultaneously as *limits* upon our thought, not merely shaping but also reducing our sense of the possible terrain of knowledge and argument. This can be a problem when certain binaries become entrenched as supposed realities, or "reified," as we theorists like to say; and so the job of the deconstructive critic is to remind us that these reified binaries are never more than a conceptual shorthand, and that sometimes they do more harm than good, by making it difficult to see the larger world of possibility that falls outside their limits. The value of a deconstructive intervention, then, is not that it can help us to transcend binary thought entirely (a perhaps wishful enterprise) but rather that it can push us to reimagine all-too familiar categories of opposition, to see what they might have concealed and excluded. To deconstruct the binary of man/woman, for example, is not to do away permanently with either concept so much as to reconfigure both; it is to recognize that if our understanding of one term undergoes a shift or transformation, then so must our understanding of the other. Or, more accurately still, it is to recognize that our idea of the *difference* between such paired terms can change, and may even temporarily vanish, as we become more aware of the characteristics common to both, and the world that belongs to neither.

Far from being the unique province of contemporary academics, deconstructive ideas can emerge at different moments in history, in any form of human endeavor. In fact, some ideas may be *inherently* deconstructive, to the degree that in their very positing they trouble what might otherwise appear fundamental (or at least rhetorically essential) binarisms. For example, within the apophatic theological tradition, the concept of God is inherently deconstructive; for by asserting that God is knowable only as that which cannot be known, negative theologians undo the opposition between knowledge and faith.

I regard Wonder Woman as just such an inherently deconstructive concept, and in the pages that follow, I attempt to say why.[6]

First, I offer a brief consideration of Wonder Woman's Amazon heritage and its implications for the character. Then I consider how her first writer, psychologist William Moulton Marston, self-consciously designed Wonder Woman to change perceptions of gender and sexuality by inverting the hierarchical oppositions of man/woman, power/ weakness, and dominance/submission. I read some of Marston's academic work in close detail, laying out the most salient aspects of his psychological theories (which remain poorly understood, even among comic book historians). I also consider several of his early *Wonder Woman* stories as reflections of those theories, and in the process, I show how these stories confront the reader with erotic energies that more conventional superhero fantasies of the era concealed, excluded, and disavowed. I then reflect briefly on the ways in which Marston's intentions have been misunderstood and misrepresented by many commentators, before showing how his own efforts to defend his work from criticism led him into some paradoxical spiritual territory (possibly to his own surprise). Finally, in the last two sections of the chapter, I turn to contemporary feminist theologian, Sarah Coakley, to consider the role of submission in a more overtly religious (Christian) context. Placing Coakley side-by-side with Marston's Wonder Woman, I raise the question of whether the idea of sexual submission can ever be fully separated from our understanding of spiritual surrender.

2

Wonder Woman's deconstructive energies derive in part from her status as the most successful modern version of a venerable mythic archetype—the Amazon. Legends about aggressive all-female tribes and their Warrior-Queens can be found in ancient literature from several different regions of the world. Whether these tales have a basis in fact is probably a matter of irresolvable dispute; but it should be fairly uncontroversial to say that the earliest Amazon stories were male-authored, and probably tell us more about the fantasies, wishes, and fears of those authors than they do about any historical reality. Consider, for example, the mythological encounter between Hercules and the Amazons—the ninth of his famous twelve labors, in the tradition established by pseudo-Apollodorus in the *Bibliotheca*—wherein the great strongman defeats the Amazon Queen Hippolyta in battle and carries off her "golden belt," a gift from the Gods symbolizing her authority. Nowadays, it is perhaps too easy to interpret this myth as a thinly veiled allegory designed to allay male fears about uppity women through the celebration of rape.[7] Equally unpleasant is the fate of Hippolyta's sister, Penthesilea, who fought on the losing side in the Trojan War; during their battle, Achilles falls in love with the Amazon warrior—but only *after* he has killed her.[8] The implication that dead women are more desirable than live ones—at least, in the mind of the most famous warrior-male in all Western culture—seems hard to escape. Certainly, one might spend some time unpacking the relationship between desire and anxiety that is at once baldly exposed and bluntly resolved in this story.

At these and other moments in her textual history the Amazon warrior might seem to have been evoked only so that the threatening female agency she symbolizes can be violently negated. But as critic Kathryn Schwartz has observed, "introducing female bodies into [hetero-male] narcissistic strategies of representation has complicated results."[9] "At once masculine and female, mistaken for men and looked at as women, Amazons generate desire between men, between women, between women and men."[10] And as a site of multiple and conflicting desires, the Amazon is also inevitably a site of multiple and conflicting meanings. This wider signifying power of the Amazon is readily apparent in the burgeoning semantic register of the term *Amazon*. Few words have been assigned such a bewildering variety of etymological roots, and these different assignments have different gendered and political inflections. For example, the idea that "Amazon" derives from the Greek "*a-mazos*" meaning "without a breast"—and the accompanying claim that Amazons mutilated themselves in order to fire their bows—seems indelibly printed upon the popular imagination, despite the fact that most modern scholars consider it false.[11] (The notion surely persists in part because it serves the prejudices of patriarchy to depict the warrior-woman as a perverse creature, ritualistically engaging in the literal violation of her own nature.) Other proposed etymologies (from Greek, Slavic, Old Iranian, Hebrew, and Phoenician) include the various senses of "unapproachable," "manless," "mannish," "warrior," "excellent woman," "fallen woman," and "mother-lord."[12] And in modern American English, the meanings of "Amazon" are no less diverse. To quote Schwartz once again:

> Wearing . . . a T-Shirt that says "Amazon" in a gay pride parade is not the same thing as being featured in a documentary called *Modern Amazons*, which is not the same thing as belonging to a rock group called The Amazons, which is not the same thing as being called an Amazon during a domestic disagreement. In this limited range of examples, the term might mean "lesbian," "feminist," "tall," "loud," or "bitch," and although it's true that . . . these terms are far from mutually exclusive, they are far from equation as well.[13]

In sum, the figure of the Amazon can elicit complex forms of identification in both men and women, at once permitting warrior-males to see themselves as women, and encouraging women to imagine themselves in terms normatively reserved for warrior-males. That these cross-identifications might further allow a man to imagine himself an object of male desire, or a woman to imagine herself an object of female desire, should be obvious. Thus, when regarded from within the paradigm of the Amazonian fantasy, a fundamental conceptual binary of human culture—the opposition of man and woman—can appear less absolute, even as the modern presumption of heterosexuality becomes questionable. Although the Amazon might function as a projection of male narcissism and sexual anxiety in certain incarnations, the significations of this fantasy figure cannot be reduced to that narcissism and anxiety alone.

Wonder Woman has inherited the irreducibility of her classical ancestors. For while it is certainly possible to point to images and storylines from the course of her 70-year career that reproduce her as a heterosexist cliché, she cannot be contained within those terms. The Amazon fantasy is simply too volatile, too sexually ambiguous, and too politically charged. William Moulton Marston, Wonder Woman's first writer, undoubtedly recognized this volatility, and utilized it.[14] For where most early comic book creators were content simply to cash in on the latest kids' craze, Marston had larger ambitions. If we take his own claims at face value, then his ultimate project was no less grandiose than the founding of a more peaceful and just society through the reformation of heterosexuality.

3

Marston is without doubt one of the most intriguing figures ever to have worked in the American comic book industry. In the early 1940s, the demographics of the profession skewed toward young men from recent immigrant families—often Jewish or Catholic in faith—from New York City and its immediate environs.[15] A significant number of these men entered the field from right out of high school. (Some future giants, including Joe Kubert of *Sgt. Rock* fame, and Carmine Infantino, the definitive artist on DC's *The Flash*, began working in comics *before* they left school.) Marston stands out, then, as a highly educated middle-aged WASP from a distinguished Massachusetts family—a Harvard graduate with multiple qualifications including a degree in law and a PhD in psychology. His doctoral dissertation, which he defended in 1921, was entitled "Systolic Blood Pressure and Reaction Time Symptoms of Deception and Constituent Mental States"; this work played a crucial role in the development of the polygraph machine, and from about 1930 on Marston started describing himself as the "inventor of the lie detector."[16] He used these credentials to generate a measure of notoriety and income by writing pop-psychology pieces for several magazines (using his polygraph to "prove" that brunettes were more emotional than blondes, for example), along with self-help books with such upbeat titles as *You Can Be Popular* and *Try Living!* A shameless shill, he even appeared with his polygraph machine in newspaper advertisements selling Gillette razors.[17] But the product that Marston most assiduously promoted was himself—in the role of "consulting psychologist" for a variety of media outlets (including, briefly, Universal Pictures).

Marston might therefore be counted among the first of a new breed of minor celebrity, the "public professional": the 1930s equivalent of a Dr. Phil or Dr. Drew.[18] But in contrast to his modern counterparts—or so I presume—Marston's private life was quite unconventional. From the late 1920s until his death in 1947, he lived in a polyamorous relationship with two women: Elizabeth Holloway (whom he married in the early 1920s) and Olive Byrne (whom he met later that decade). Each woman had two children by him, and according to all accounts, the bonds of affection between all three partners were strong; Elizabeth named her daughter after Olive, and the two women continued to live together for another 30 years after Marston's death. This arrangement, unusual in any period of American history, might justly earn Marston the designation of sexual radical. (Olive Byrne was herself well-acquainted with sexual controversy, as the devoted niece of birth-control pioneer Margaret Sanger.) Certainly, if these facts had become widely known, he would have faced a career-damaging scandal. But if Marston was concerned about this possibility he did not record it, and at least as far as his private life was concerned he seems largely to have avoided moral censure (although his work on Wonder Woman would not entirely escape such condemnation).[19]

It was in his capacity as roving "mental health expert" for various women's magazines that Marston first drew the attention of the comic book industry, probably with an article entitled "What Comics Do to Your Children," published in a periodical called *Your Life*, in 1939. Marston had no truck with the arguments of the more rabid anti-comics crusaders of the era, but he was not an uncritical cheerleader for the new form, either; significantly, he castigated the industry wide tendency to depict women as "jealous, mercenary, and moronic," and also suggested that concerned parents might organize a Cleaner Comics League.[20] This piece seems to have caught the eye of pioneer comics publisher, M. C. Gaines, of the All American Comics Company. Like his friend and business partner, Jack Liebowitz (see previous chapter), Gaines feared an anti-comics backlash, and was keen to recruit respectable experts such as Marston to serve on an "advisory board" in a public relations capacity. Marston responded to his overtures, and was soon writing more positive articles about comic books, and singling out M. C. Gaines as one of the most intelligent publishers in the business.[21]

But Marston had more to offer than his professional endorsement. Comics had become one of the boom industries of the decade—and he wanted a piece of the action. Which is not to say that he was simply being opportunistic when he pitched Gaines his idea for a female superhero. Even his first article on comic books praised the emotional immediacy of the medium, and as a subsequent article in *The American Scholar* shows, Marston saw a remarkable potential in the form as a whole. These claims still make thought provoking reading more than 50 years later:

> This phenomenal development of a national comics addiction puzzles professional educators and leaves the literary critics gasping. Comics scorn finesse, thereby incurring the wrath of linguistic adepts. They defy the limits of accepted fact and convention, thus amortizing to apoplexy the ossified arteries of routine thought. But by these very tokens the picture-story fantasy cuts loose the hampering debris of art and artifice and touches the tender spots

of universal human desires and aspirations, hidden customarily beneath long accumulated protective coverings of indirection and disguise. Comics speak, without qualm or sophistication, to the innermost ears of the wishful self.[22]

It's probably safe to say that no one else in the comic industry at the time could have articulated this position in this way—even if they had believed it. But the idea that comics pierce the layers of the civilized ego to touch the core of the human self was far from being the most unusual of Marston's theories; and other, bolder notions would come through in the *Wonder Woman* comics he wrote for Gaines during the next few years.

There isn't much to indicate just how radical some of Marston's ideas were in the first appearance of his new character, in *All Star Comics* #8 (December, 1941). But from the beginning, Wonder Woman was a different kind of superhero. Unlike the origin stories of Superman, Batman, The Flash, The Green Lantern, and so many others, Wonder Woman's debut takes place not in the "real" America of the period, but in an entirely fantasized space called Paradise Island—the uncharted tropical home of the Amazons. The idyllic routine of this all-female community is disrupted when a pilot from the US air force named Steve Trevor literally crashes into the picture, to be rescued from his plane by the beautiful Princess Diana. He is the first man she has ever seen, and—rather like Shakespeare's Miranda in *The Tempest*—the young Princess immediately falls in love with this new arrival, much to the consternation of her mother, Queen Hippolyta.[23] Denying Diana access to the fallen pilot, she takes this opportunity to reveal the history of Paradise Island and the secret of the Amazons' great strength to her daughter.

At this point the comic takes on a formal distinctiveness to match the content, as Marston, still an inexperienced comic writer, turns to the medium of illustrated prose to tell an adapted version of the myth of Hercules and Hippolyta. In his account, Hippolyta and her Amazon tribe escaped from slavery under Hercules through the intercession of Aphrodite, the Goddess of Love, and established an isolated all-female community. Utilizing various gifts of the gods, including a magic sphere that allows them to survey events in "man's world," the Amazons have access to all of the technologies of modern culture, while retaining the mystical knowledge of the ancients. As a result, they have wisdom and physical abilities far beyond those of ordinary men and women. However, they continue to wear their bracelets as a reminder of their former error in submitting to male rule, and Aphrodite has decreed that if any Amazon allows a man to chain her hands she will lose her powers. (Given the absence of a man to serve as a father, Diana's status as Hippolyta's daughter is not explained at first; but a year later, in *Wonder Woman* #1, we are told that Diana's very life is a gift of the gods. Molded from clay by her Amazon mother, and infused with a soul by Aphrodite herself, Wonder Woman's origin is therefore also a fantasy of parthenogenesis, with no male intercession whatsoever—a relatively rare phenomenon in the annals of popular culture and high culture alike.)[24]

Aphrodite and Athena then appear to Hippolyta and tell her that she cannot remain neutral in the struggle between America and the Nazis, because America is "the last citadel of democracy, and of equal rights for women." Hippolyta therefore decides to hold a competition to find the strongest of the Amazons to go with Steve to the United States, but out of possessive affection she forbids her daughter to compete. Moved by her love for Steve, Diana disobeys, enters the competition disguised, and emerges victorious. Hippolyta accepts the result, and gives Diana a costume to wear in her new home, based on the familiar US nationalist symbols of eagle and flag—and thus an American feminist icon is born![25]

4

That Marston was a sincere advocate of women's liberation is readily apparent in this first story, with its depiction of a peaceful, advanced, all-female culture, and its explicit association of women's rights with American values. But as the series progressed it became increasingly clear that Marston was at least equally interested in using his character to promulgate his own theories about gender, sexuality, and personality types. Marston had previously expounded on these theories at great length in several popular and academic texts; but they are given most elaborate expression in his *magnum opus* in the field of the human sciences, a weighty tome with what is to contemporary ears a somewhat unintentionally comedic title: *The Emotions of Normal People.*[26]

Four hundred pages in length, filled with "technical" terms and concepts of Marston's own invention, and freely mixing neuroscience with anthropology, sociology, psychoanalysis, unsourced anecdotes, and wildly speculative leaps, this book can be a frustrating read.[27] Throughout, Marston blurs crucial distinctions between emotional categories, behavioral tendencies, states of consciousness, and external stimuli, with predictably confusing results; and despite his avowed intent "to define timeworn emotional terms with greater exactness or scientific meaning than that employed by literary men," he often employs "conventional definitions of behavior, . . . literary language, and . . . social and cultural stereotypes about sex and race" when attempting to explain his ideas, as Geoffrey C. Bunn has noted.[28] Consequently, *The Emotions of Normal People* fails to cohere. Some passages simply defy intelligibility; others are very hard going. But Marston's work remains curiously fascinating, and even admirable when considered in the historical contexts of both the discipline of psychology, and conventional attitudes toward sexual morality.[29]

Marston's central thesis, baldly stated, is that all human sexual, social, and political interactions can be explained in terms of the opposition between the "primary emotions" of "dominance" and "submission."[30] As far as general claims about human behavior go, this probably would not have sounded terribly shocking in many intellectual circles of the period. Variations on the position were familiar and even fashionable, in the form of sub-Nietzschean philosophizing about the primacy of the will-to-power, pseudo-Freudian chatter about the "natural" instinct for aggression, and crude Social Darwinist arguments justifying the existence of poverty, or the oppression of women and minorities on the grounds of their "innate" inferiority. But Marston was perhaps unusual in refusing to grant the most conservative implications of his premise. Although his examples sometimes reveal that he believed stereotypes we now regard as essentialist at best, and sexist and racist at worst—he was not untouched by the prejudices of his era—he nevertheless strongly resisted the idea that nature's plan doomed the majority of the species to lives of suffering and oppression. Instead, he believed that psychology could teach us to overcome our more aggressive and self-destructive tendencies. Thus, as Bunn writes: "From an epistemology that appeared merely to condone women's inferior social position, Marston attempted to construct a psychology of freedom."[31]

Marston's transformation of the "primary emotions" of dominance and submission into the building blocks for a project of liberation begins with his research into certain sorority games then popular at Jackson College, the sister school of Tufts University. Marston was particularly fascinated by something called a "baby party," a freshman initiation ritual "so named because the freshmen girls were required to dress like babies" and submit to the demands of their senior sisters. Here is Marston's description of one such event:

> At the party, the freshmen girls were put through various stunts under command of the sophomores. Upon one occasion . . . the freshmen girls were led into a dark corridor where their eyes were blindfolded, and their arms were bound behind them. Only one freshman at a time was taken through this corridor along which sophomore guards were stationed at intervals. This arrangement was designed to impress the girls punished with the impossibility of escape from their captresses. After a series of harmless punishments, each girl was led into a large room where all the Junior and Senior girls were assembled. There she was sentenced to go through various exhibitions, supposed to be especially suitable to punish each girl's particular failures to submit to discipline imposed by the upper class girls. The sophomore girls carried long sticks with which to enforce, if necessary, the stunts the freshmen were required to perform . . . frequent rebellion of the freshmen against the commands of their captresses and guards furnished the most exciting portion of the entertainment according to the report of the majority of the upper class girls.
>
> Nearly all the sophomores reported excited pleasantness of captivation emotion throughout the party. The pleasantness . . . appeared to increase when they were obliged to overcome rebellious freshmen physically . . .[32]

As an account of 1920s sorority life, this might seem intriguing enough! But the element that most engaged Marston's attention is what he here calls "pleasant captivation emotion." In the immediate context, it is hard to interpret this as anything other than a euphemized description for the erotic stimulation felt by the dominant party in a light bondage game—something Marston claims "nearly all" of the sophomore girls experienced. Marston goes on to contrast this "pleasant captivation emotion" with what he calls the "passion emotion" of the freshman girls, and which he defines further as "an extremely pleasant feeling of being subjected and made more and more helpless in the hands of an allied stimulus person of superior strength"; again, this sounds like a euphemism for sexual arousal, this time at the experience of submission.[33] Marston concludes (on the basis of a survey) that three-quarters of the freshman girls experienced this "pure pleasant passion emotion" during the "baby party."

Marston attempts to distinguish these feelings of "pleasant captivation emotion" (which he also calls "active love") and "passion emotion" (or "passive love") from sado-masochism, a concept that clearly has unhealthy connotations for him. For example, he insists that the dominant parties in the game he describes are always oriented toward the submissive party's pleasure and well-being, unlike real sadists.[34] His notion of "pure" or "true" captivation emotion is therefore delightfully paradoxical, a kind of domination-that-is-not-domination, "a reaction during which the subject must be wholly controlled by alliance with the interests of the person captivated."[35] Nevertheless, Marston's description of the "pleasant" emotions generated by the "baby party" could quite easily be interpreted as—or confused with — a kind of BDSM idyll, in which dominant and submissive partners are so perfectly synchronized that their relationship becomes a perfect dialectic: the dominant "bottoming-from-the-top," as it were, while the submissive "tops-from-the-bottom." But the question of whether Marston's account of the dialectic of "captivation" and "passion" emotion can finally be distinguished from an idealized BDSM scenario may be less important than the conclusions he draws from his research about the different capacities for "pure passion emotion" in males and females.

Although Marston seems less interested in the hazing rituals of boys' fraternities, spending far less time in their analysis, he does briefly contrast them with the games of the girls. He claims that boys "seldom, if ever," elicit "pure passion emotion" in one another—except "in one especial situation," when the older boys put the juniors through their "exhibitions" in front of a girls' dormitory, "to the great excitement of the girls, who watched the performance from the . . . windows." From this he concludes, with one of his typical leaps, "[t]hat strong passion emotion could be evoked from a majority of the boys studied, by girls who made the boys captive in the same way they treated the freshman girls, provided that girls could be found of sufficient strength, emotional or physical, to impress themselves upon the male subjects[.]"[36]

With remarkable rapidity, Marston extrapolates to the further conclusion that, for a combination of physiological and psychological reasons, men are more disposed to the experience of "true passion emotion"—that is, pleasure in submission—than to "true captivation emotion," or dominance.[37] However, since men are also disposed to confuse "love" with "appetite" (something that Marston asserts more than he explains), the average male—at least in the West—denies himself this pleasure of passionate submission.[38] (In one of his more jaw-dropping asides, Marston declares that things are different "in the Orient, where love is practiced as an art, [and] the necessity of woman's complete control of physical love behavior is recognized freely, no matter whether the woman be wife or slave girl.") No less provocative than his argument that most men are inclined to repress their "natural" desire to be dominated, however, is his argument that women are equally capable of taking pleasure in both "captivation emotion" *and* "passion emotion," and are therefore "naturally" capable of enjoying both dominant and submissive roles in both heterosexual and lesbian relationships. Consequently, many women are as inclined to lesbianism as heterosexuality; Marston suggests that the figure is as high as one-in-two.

Marston seems to anticipate resistance from his audience on this point, telling us that before he undertook his research, he had "not the slightest idea . . . of the prevalence of [sexual] relationships among women," and that he was surprised to discover "that nearly half of the female love relationships concerning which significant data could be found, were accompanied by bodily love stimulation."[39] Of course, what this actually means statistically in terms of the general population is anyone's guess, since Marston does not elaborate on the sources of his data. Instead, he supplements the claim with the following striking anecdote:

A male psychologist once reported to me a case of two girl lovers, who had been separated from one another for some weeks by the college authorities. These girls performed the love act unhesitatingly in his presence, manifesting intense passion and captivation emotion respectively. According to this report, the girls regarded their love relationship as something peculiarly sacred, and though they were both reported as forming love relationships with males shortly after this occurrence, these relationships with men did not appear to detract in any way from their love for one another.

Marston declares this instance—supposedly reported to him by a fellow professional who just happens to use the same technical terms—to be merely an unusually uninhibited example of "a general trend of female love relationships of this type," and concludes:

> So long as a woman possesses two distinct love mechanisms [that is, the capacity to experience both passion and captivation emotion], both stimulable from the environment by stimulus persons of different types, it seems highly probably that she will continue to enjoy both types of love relationship whenever possible, despite attempted social prohibition . . . Other cases of captivation-passion relationships between girls which have been reported to me, where medical examinations were available . . . no emotional or physical results of a deleterious nature could be detected.[40]

If most men secretly desire to be dominated by women (howsoever they might disavow those feelings), while most women are capable of enjoying the experience of both domination *and* submission, with men *and* with each other, then the sexual mores of Marston's society were entirely at odds with the natural order of things: a recipe for human misery. A considerable program of sexual retraining was obviously called for, and according to Marston, only women could do the job.[41]

Marston therefore proposes a utopian project of "Emotional Re-Education" in the final pages of his book. In this vision, the most "advanced" women in society must become "Love Leaders," teaching both men and other women to take greater pleasure in submission, through their "love supremacy."

> . . . the training of males and less actively developed women in passion response [sic] to the active love leaders, must be left to woman herself. No task could be found more compatible with woman's normal emotional equipment, once its normalcy is publicly acknowledged. But woman must be taught to use her love power exclusively for the benefit of humanity and not for her own destructive, appetitive gratifications, as so many women are doing under the present appetitive regime.[42]

To evoke a cliché familiar from almost every superhero origin story: "powers such as these must be used for the good of mankind." If nothing else, then, *The Emotions of Normal People* makes clear that the fantasy of a beautiful woman saving the world through the power of erotic love was central to Marston's thinking by 1928—thirteen years before Wonder Woman made her first appearance.

5

I suspect that few people have developed a more intellectually convoluted or politically optimistic analysis of the light bondage games of sorority girls than William Moulton Marston's *The Emotions of Normal People*. But, as complex and circular as some of his theories are, his argument basically boils down to a fairly simple two-part manifesto: the world will become a better place when men learn to take pleasure in sexual submission, as most women have already learned to do; and the best teachers of men in this regard will be "actively developed," dominant-but-kind women who are willing to serve as their "Love Leaders." And besides being designed to promote traditional feminism, Marston's *Wonder Woman* comics were also an imaginative vehicle for this more idiosyncratic and paradoxical vision of a world in which women learn to serve through dominance, so that men can be liberated through submission. As a result, they remain to this day some of the most curious, engaging, and genuinely sexually daring superhero comics ever written. In almost every story from these first few years, conventional themes of female empowerment are developed alongside frequent and sometimes unmistakably salacious images of bondage—all offered in the playful and essentially pain-free context of a wildly fantastic cartoon world in which the impossible and the magical veer into the downright surreal.

For example, in just her third appearance in *Sensation Comics* #2, Diana foils the plans of a small Nazi army that has somehow hidden itself in a remote part of the United States. Significantly, she does so with the help of a group of sorority girls from Holiday University, led by Etta Candy—a happily overweight-but-glamorous dominatrix figure who soon became a regular supporting character. The celebration of "girl power" is fairly obvious throughout the story; "Who's afraid of a man?" the girls shout, in the manner of eager cheerleaders, when Wonder Woman warns them of the dangers they face. "If they're men, we can catch them!"[43] Only slightly less obvious, however, is the suggestion that it can be fun to struggle with bonds. When the Nazis briefly capture Diana in her civilian guise as a nurse they tie her up to prevent her raising the alarm. Breaking free just one panel later, she announces, "They should have used chains—it would have been more fun breaking them." This somewhat wistful desire to be tied up with something more substantial is just a hint of things to come in future issues—as is the brief scene on the final page of the story, wherein Etta Candy spanks Dr. Poison, the evil female leader of the Nazis, with a paddle. [44]

In the following issue, Marston returned to the girls of Holiday University with a story about a young woman named Eve who has been seduced into working for the Nazis by a handsome German spy. Wonder Woman and Etta Candy catch Eve before she can do any real harm and, in an obvious echo of Marston's research at Jackson College, Etta and her sisters induct the unfortunate girl into their sorority. Her hazing involves being blindfolded, forced to kneel to catch some actual candy in her mouth (held suspended on a string by Etta), and spanked when she fails—an experience that leaves her less vulnerable to the charms of handsome Nazis!

Unable to leave the spectacle of sorority spankings alone, Marston returns to the education of Eve the next month, too; in *Sensation Comics* #4 she is again depicted being beaten on the backside while kneeling before Etta (who now sits on a raised chair like a throne, issuing orders like an empress), in an episode that is presented as part of the normal routine of her sorority life (see Figure 2.1). In the subsequent panel, Eve is chained to the radiator by means of a dog collar; significantly, she does not object to any of this treatment, although she does express mild annoyance when she is unable to assist Steve Trevor in capturing some Nazis as a result ("Darn this dog-collar anyway!")[45] The context (which increasingly seems more of a pretext) is a plot about a Nazi kidnapping ring. The leader of the Nazis is once again female, the villainous Baronness Von Gunther; she has a penchant for dressing like Cleopatra and making her victims serve her as slaves—and since all her victims are female, too, this provides Marston and his artist, H. G. Peter, with an opportunity to present a scene in which several scantily dressed girls are forced to march in high-step by a blond Fraulein wielding a whip. "This teaches girls discipline," says the Baroness to Wonder Woman. "Tomorrow you will join their ranks!" It's unclear how arch Wonder Woman is being when she responds: "Won't I have fun?"[46]

It's also unclear how much of an impact these scenes had upon sales figures—but those were *very* good indeed. By just the third issue, *Sensation Comics* was reported to be selling over half a million

Figure 2.1 From *Sensation Comics* #4, a typical depiction of sorority life as imagined by William Marston and H. G. Peter. © DC Comics.

copies per month.[47] Perhaps emboldened by this success, Marston started to mix ever more explicit arguments for the pleasures of bondage in with his feminist messages. In *Sensation Comics* #6, for example, Diana returns to Paradise Island for a visit. She arrives in time to participate in the apparently traditional Amazon sport of "girl roping." Riding around an arena on the backs of their giant kangaroos (you may have missed the appearance of these creatures in Herodotus), the Amazon girls attempt to lasso one another, pull one another down, and tie one another up. Wonder Woman, it turns out, is a champion girl-roper. After reading this slightly surreal page-and-half-long celebration of girl-girl bondage-play-as-public-recreation on Paradise Island, one might easily overlook the fact that Diana is presented with one of her most famous weapons, her gold lasso of truth, in this particular story.[48]

Three months later, in *Sensation Comics* #9, Diana trades places with a look-alike, a woman whose husband feels threatened by her desire to work outside the home. The feminist point is obviously that women should be allowed to enter the workforce; but this message competes with the spectacle of Wonder Woman enjoying the pretence of submitting to the demands of a chauvinist husband, even as he chains her to the stove.[49]

Then, in November 1942, toward the end of his first year writing the character, Marston published one of most surreal and ambitious stories of his tenure to date. Appearing in *Sensation Comics* #11, it explores the pleasures of submission more overtly than any previous tale, and also lays out Marston's thesis of "love leadership" clearly— if perhaps not entirely seriously. The adventure is presented as a kind of dream sequence, a journey undertaken by Etta, Steve, and Diana's ectoplasmic forms while they are asleep. As such, it's one of the more hallucinatory stories of Marston's early career, inspiring some of Peter's most imaginative artwork—the panel in which Wonder Woman, Steve, and Etta leave their bodies makes for a particularly nice piece of proto-psychedelia. They travel to a planet named Eros, which can be taken as an early hint as to Marston's intentions to expound upon the nature of "active love" in this story. Eros is a female-dominated world where the culture of submission is so successfully internalized that most residents enjoy long periods of what they call imprisonment—although the prisons are more like vocational boarding schools, and certainly not conceived as punitive institutions. In one of these prisons we meet a native Eros girl named Rebla. She has blossomed in this strange system, spending many happy hours inventing new machines in the prison workshop, and dancing at "prison parties." She also enjoys the game of "Man-Fishing" (see Figure 2.2) during her recreational periods. (This fabulous sequence is absolutely as weird as it sounds. Rebla and her friends are

Figure 2.2 Marston's comics are also notable for the surreal quality of sequences such as this one from *Sensation Comics* #11. © DC Comics.

depicted sitting on the gracefully curving walls of an arena, holding giant fishing rods and "casting" for muscular, Grecian-featured men who are dressed in a curious uniform of short-pants, boots, and polka-dot undershirts. Marston's caption tells us: "Rebla's superior strength made her champion—she could land any man in the prison.")[50]

However, Rebla is ultimately forced to leave the prison and take up a leadership position in her society. She protests, proclaiming: "I am not fit to rule! I hate responsibility—I like to submit, to be told what to do!" But her feelings are ignored, and she is "condemned to freedom . . . to serve indefinitely as ruler of Trans Mountania." Resentfully, Rebla rebels, overthrowing the Eros government, and capturing Wonder Woman with a paralyzing ray of her own invention in the process. She then places a man named Dominus in charge, before sending herself back to prison!

Unfortunately, because Dominus and his men run these prisons, they are less pleasant than the female-controlled institutions in which Rebla once thrived (and yes, these sequences provide an opportunity for some more imagery of a woman in chains, threatened with whipping). Steve Trevor breaks free of his guards but he is unable to free Wonder Woman; instead, on her instructions, he releases Rebla, who has by now realized her mistake, and it is Rebla who helps Wonder Woman recover from the effects of the paralyzing ray. Wonder Woman then restores order, rapidly and easily. Plucking Dominus from the throne of Eros with one hand, she appears to slap him around the face with the other, announcing, "little boys with big mouths must have them stopped up!" (While close enough to a conventional superheroic smack-down, the invocation of "little boys" probably carries an implication that men-who-would-be-dominant merely need a strong enough "Mummy" figure to put them in their place.) The rightful female ruler of Eros acknowledges her error in selecting Rebla for a leadership position and sends her back to a female-run prison, to everyone's joy.

Of course, readers at the time could have enjoyed "Journey to Planet Eros" as a kind of "bizzaro" tale, without knowing Marston's work in *The Emotions of Normal People*. But in the light of that text, the story obviously takes on a quite specific resonance as a tongue-in-cheek fantasy about the challenges of "love leadership." Although smart, strong, and capable, Rebla simply cannot overcome her preference for submissive roles, and is ready to fight to stay in chains. Marston suggests that she should not be judged too negatively for this—it was a mistake for her matriarchal ruler to thrust responsibilities upon her for which she was emotionally unsuited—but of course Wonder Woman, by contrast, has no such problem asserting her authority to restore a happy order. She is consequently able to save Eros from a grim future under the dictatorship of a "selfish-dominant" male (who, in an obvious nod toward Marston's published theories, is given the un-subtle name of Dominus). The opposition between Rebla and Wonder Woman is clearly intended to make Wonder Woman's take-charge stance attractive to Marston's more submissively inclined female readers (and Marston would use a variation on this device several more times in his career). The story also plays up the contrast between Steve, the heroic male who openly adores a powerful woman, and the selfishly dominant men of Eros. "You Eros boys have a lot to learn!" Steve announces, when taking one of them down. The implication seems to be that Steve's desire for Wonder Woman does not make him less manly, while the desire of the Eros "boys" to rule instead of serve their dominant-but-wise female leaders is marked as immature. (Steve is often dismissed as little more than a male Lois to Wonder Woman's Superman, whose presence is more a result of the formulaic requirements of the genre than any original creative purpose; but in this story, at least, his job is also to communicate that men can be as attracted and inspired as women by Wonder Woman's power and assertiveness. "Real men *like* strong women," he reminds us.)

But Rebla's failure to rise to the level of "love leader" also suggests Marston's awareness that his fantasy world might not appeal to everyone. I described the story as tongue-in-cheek, but there may be a slightly poignant note here, too. It's almost as if Marston's acknowledging, 14 years after his call for a generation of female "love leaders" to guide humanity out of the darkness and into the light, just what a burden his fantasy places on the shoulders of those women. "Who'd be a love leader," Rebla seems to ask, "when it's just so much more fun to be dominated?"

6

I could offer much more in this vein, providing descriptions of other stories from Marston's tenure that push the envelope with regard to images of bondage and promote his thesis about the joys and benefits of submission. For lack of space, I must regretfully pass over a close reading of the stories featuring Reform Island, for example—an Amazon-run holding facility for criminals located near Paradise Island, where the prisoners wear "Venus Girdles," magical devices that render even the most selfish criminals receptive to the joys of service. (Interested readers are invited to consult DC's splendid *Wonder Woman* archive collections for these sequences, and more.) Instead, some reflection on the obvious question of how these scenes have been interpreted seems in order.

Many commentators assume that Marston's interest in erotic bondage is simply incompatible with a sincerely held belief in women's equality, or indeed with feminist politics in general. For example, Douglas Wolk writes that, "as conceived by . . . Marston, . . . [*Wonder Woman*] was very specifically an excuse for stories about sexual domination and submission . . . [but] After a certain point, that didn't wash," and so in the 1970s the character was made over as a series "about the feminist movement."[51] The implication is that because Marston's stories are "about sexual domination" they couldn't also be about feminism; *that* came later. But Wolk at least allows Marston the courage of his convictions. Richard Reynolds won't even give him that much; he flatly accuses Marston of "disingenuously" developing the "appearance and costume" of the character as a "frank appeal to male fantasies of sexual domination."[52] These remarks are problematic for several reasons. Besides accusing Marston of lying (on the basis of what actually seems a very limited acquaintance with his work), Reynolds makes the sexist and homophobic mistake of assuming that only men could find Wonder Woman's appearance sexually appealing, or have an interest in "sexual domination." But as we have seen, the chief burden of Marston's academic writing was to show that women "naturally" enjoyed erotic bondage scenarios in which they could take the positions of Top and Bottom relatively interchangeably, without requiring the presence of a man at all.

Moreover, neither Reynolds nor Wolk would seem to have a way of accounting for the reactions of, say, Gloria Steinem, or Trina Robbins, or Lillian S. Robinson—all of whom write persuasively about the explicitly feminist message of empowerment they took from Marston's comics. Of course, this is not to imply that these women are also unambiguous celebrants of bondage, lesbian, or otherwise. Steinem writes well about Wonder Woman and the politics of representation, the contexts of the 1940s, issues of "sisterhood," and so on; but she passes over the erotic implications of Marston's work in silence.[53] Robbins, by contrast, acknowledges the presence of the bondage scenes but downplays their significance, arguing that, "in comics from the 1940s, if the heroes weren't getting tied up so that they could escape from their bonds, their girlfriends were getting tied up so that they could be rescued by the heroes." She seems to think that other (male) critics have made too much of these scenes in *Wonder Woman* stories, and points out that Captain Marvel's Billy Batson was often bound and gagged, but she "has never read anything about bondage" in *those* comics.[54] This claim depends upon repressing everything we know about Marston's theories, of course, and also pretending that there is no difference of degree (if not in kind) between the scenes of captivity and struggle in other superhero titles and those written by Marston. It's a tall order; I defy anyone to find a sequence in the pages of Captain Marvel quite like the one in *Wonder Woman* #6, where Diana performs an escapist routine for charity: a four-page scene, in which Diana is bound, manacled, placed in a Tibetan collar, and a leather brank (we are even offered a brief history lesson on the cultural origins of these notorious restraints) and lowered into a tank of water to struggle with her bonds for several panels. Parts of the sequence frankly bear more resemblance to the work of Robert Crumb than to that of C. C. Beck.[55]

Lillian Robinson, on the other hand, is willing to treat Marston's theme of erotic bondage in detail, writing particularly well about the spanking scenes featuring Etta Candy and her sorority girls—even as she insists on the continuing relevance of Wonder Woman for feminists as "the apotheosis of the female hero."[56] Robinson's refusal to assume that the presence of bondage imagery undercuts the avowed feminism of the series is almost unique in the critical literature; she is apparently one of the very few critics willing to read Marston as he clearly hoped to be read.

These disagreements among modern readers over both the extent and the implications of Marston's sexual themes actual replicate a quarrel behind the scenes at DC Comics in the 1940s between Marston and Josette Frank, of the Child Study Association of America—a quarrel that is usefully documented in Les Daniels' book on Wonder Woman (an essential reference for any scholar of the character). A distinguished figure in the field of child education—a major annual award for children's fiction is today named after her—Frank also held a seat on M. C. Gaines's in-house advisory board for a few years. Her published work indicates that she was actually quite open-minded about the educational value of comics, in contrast with most "child-centered" commentators of the period. But she disliked Marston's *Wonder Woman* stories intensely, regarding them as "sadistic" and inappropriate for younger readers, and she would ultimately resign from her advisory position in 1944, on the grounds that her repeated criticisms of the strip were not being taken seriously.[57]

Marston repudiated Frank's accusation of sadism with a variation on the argument he had made previously in *The Emotions of Normal People*; since the Amazons of Paradise Island enjoyed the experience of "confinement," they were not being sadistic when they tied each other up. Importantly, however, Marston did not deny the erotic charge of these scenes; on the contrary, in several letters defending his work to his publisher, M. C. Gaines, he insisted that the experience of titillation was an essential factor in his program of social education. In non-academic prose, he laid out his theory regarding the common but disavowed desire of males to be sexually mastered by women, and explained that Wonder Woman was designed to evoke that feeling in male readers, in the name of a happier future for all humankind. "The only hope for peace is to teach people who are full of pep and unbound force to enjoy being bound," he insisted, adding that "Women are exciting for this one reason—it is the secret of women's allure—women enjoy submission, being bound. This I bring out in the Paradise Island sequences where the girls beg for chains and enjoy wearing them."[58]

Les Daniels must be commended for making the details of this argument public; since the publication of his book it has become much harder to dismiss the "bondage scenes" in *Wonder Woman* as mere conventions of the genre.[59] But even Daniels presents Marston's self-justifications as inconsistent and potentially disingenuous. After all, he observes, if Marston's purpose was to encourage heterosexual men to embrace their inner desire to be mastered by women, then why were Diana and her friends always the ones getting tied up—or tying one another up—in these stories? "Could [Marston] have been deliberately using the titillating idea of women in bondage to lure chauvinistic male readers into stories that demonstrated female superiority?" Daniels asks, positing an elaborate sexual game of bait-and-switch. Unable to resolve these questions, he rhetorically throws up his hands, and concludes by suggesting that the whole debate was just impossibly confusing and perhaps a bit silly: "Twenty years later editor Sheldon Mayer was still talking about [the phallic symbolism of] submarines and trying to make sense of it all."[60]

What does not seem to have occurred to anyone in the course of these tormented efforts to "make sense" of Marston's intentions is that his scenes of lesbian bondage were aimed as much at his female audience as the straight boys.[61] But surely this normatively subversive possibility is the most likely one? After all, these stories were written by a man who lived intimately with two women; a man who had claimed in an academic context that nearly half of all female friendships were accompanied by "bodily love stimulation," and that this was perfectly healthy; and a man who provided his creation with the occasional catch-phrase, "Suffering Sappho!" Of course, Marston might well have refrained from articulating an explicit defense of lesbian desire in his letters repudiating the charges of Josette Frank. His argument about the importance of teaching boys to enjoy "restraint" was obviously less provocative. But if the girls in his audience found themselves aroused by, say, the "girl-roping" games of Paradise Island (whether from a dominant or submissive perspective), it is clear that Marston would have cheered them on. It seems important to make this point in no uncertain terms, because it establishes that theorists and critics interested in thinking about Wonder Woman as a figure of lesbian identification are not inappropriately or anachronistically projecting their own desires onto her; in fact, they are probably responding precisely as her original creator hoped they would.[62]

Another point worth emphasizing is Marston's willingness to regard the superheroic fantasy as a sexual fantasy—or perhaps more accurately, his willingness to draw out the repressed eroticism that he felt was already present in the superhero fantasy, in disavowed form. (Here Marston anticipated Alan Moore's exploration of the sexuality of superheroes in *Watchmen* by several decades.) Trina Robbins therefore has the right instinct when she invites us to compare the bondage scenes in *Wonder Woman* to those in *Captain Marvel*, even if she draws the wrong conclusions. For in displaying their erotic energies on the surface, Marston's *Wonder Woman* stories can heighten our awareness of the repressed or disavowed eroticism in other superhero comics, including the homoeroticism of those comics. But it seems to me quite perverse (so to speak) to insist that the bondage sequences in other comic books make the ones in Marston's *less* sexy; instead, after reading Marston, the entire genre might start to look more interestingly kinky.

Given Marston's recorded attitudes, I suspect he would not even have denied his own erotic pleasure in the fantasies he generated— although again, he probably would not have written about such matters to his publisher. But we can point to what may be the closest thing to "evidence" for Marston's own erotic investment in his creation by comparing a surviving copy of one of his typescripts with the story as it actually appeared, in *Sensation Comics* #20. This story is, in fact, a particularly "empowering" one, selected by Gloria Steinem for her anthology of *Wonder Woman* comics; it features a patriarchal, sexist American general who, by the end, is forced to admit that women can serve as bravely and proudly as men in the military. As part of its typically convoluted plot, however, a woman named Marva uses Wonder Woman's magic lasso against her, forcing her to take off her costume and put on Marva's WAAC uniform. Marston's typescript describes the scene in detail as follows:

> The girls are changing clothes, Marva still holding the lasso which is around WW's neck. WW has removed her costume. She is barefooted wearing Marva's panties and is fastening Marva's brazzier [sic] behind her back. Marva wears WW's bodice, pants and boots and is adjusting the headband on her head, holding the lasso in one hand as she does so. WW faces Marva and looks her over.
>
> Marva: Your costume fits me perfectly—how do I look?
> WW: Very pretty! Your looks have improved tremendously since you joined the WAACS![63]

The dialog clearly reflects Marston's desire to make female assertiveness attractive, and in the published comic, it remains the same. But H. G. Peter depicts the events rather differently; Wonder Woman is drawn from the waist up, already clothed in Marva's WAAC uniform (see Figure 2.3). Thus, where Marston's description draws attention to the fact that Wonder Woman has been leashed in her own lasso, compelled to strip naked, and then put on another woman's bra and panties, Peter's illustration leaps over all this to the moment where Wonder Woman is fully dressed again in Marva's outfit. The alteration risks creating confusion in the reader; without Marston's caption, the action would be quite obscure. Clearly someone— editor Sheldon Moldoff? M. C. Gaines? Josette Frank? H. G. Peter? Marston himself?—had second thoughts about this scene, and it was

Figure 2.3 This panel, from *Sensation Comics* #20, is rather less provocative than the scene as imagined in Marston's script. © DC Comics.

revised accordingly. But reading over Marston's description, it's hard to imagine how he ever thought such a scene would fly. He must surely have anticipated that it would have to be rendered more conservatively—but he wrote it anyway, because it was what *he* saw, or wanted to see, at this point in the story. And what he wanted to see was Wonder Woman stripping for another woman, while collared in her own lasso. For me, encountering this moment in the typescript was almost like discovering Marston peeping on his creation, if I can use such a metaphor without sounding censorious.

I'm wary of putting it this way, because Marston was not ashamed of his imagination, and I'm not trying to imply that he should have been. Of course, some might think that this kind of discovery proves Marston to be the hypocrite Reynolds takes him to be—on the assumption that a man who could enjoy fantasizing about women stripping each other and playing light bondage games could not also believe in the political goals of feminism. But Marston himself would not agree with this assumption, and neither would quite a few contemporary feminist writers.[64] Indeed, the possibility that such fantasies could be entirely compatible with progressive politics is one that

Marston's comics insistently raise—even though few of his modern critics have been willing to consider it.

Whatever you may feel about Marston's theories and intentions, it's important to grasp two main points that emerge from this discussion. First, his ideas about gender and sexuality were generally far more radical and interesting than those of some of the critics who have written about him since (many of whom do not seem able to imagine that a women might enjoy being sexually dominant, or that men might enjoy being dominated). Second, Marston was using the world of Wonder Woman as a space in which to elaborate not just his psychological theories, but also his fantasies—sometimes in a strikingly uninhibited and playful way, as we have seen. For this reason, while his theories can help us to understand the material of those fantasies, they can only take us so far; they "explain" his comic book stories only in the way that the events of a day might help us to understand a dream—without ever fully accounting for its unique form, direction, and associations.

To put it another way: we might think of Marston's comics not so much as articulations of his theories about gender but as the waking dreams of a gender theorist. In this mode of "dreaming theory," his comics gently mock the automatic responses of an over-determined, over-serious sexual culture, defusing both moral indignation and fetishistic obsession by simply refusing to grant either posture any real weight. Surreal and trippy where his theoretical writing is pedestrian and clunky, Marston's stories for *Sensation Comics* and *Wonder Woman* are therefore paradoxically less vulnerable to the charges of confusion and incoherence that his academic prose inevitably provokes; fantastic and imaginative where his psychological arguments are sometimes crudely materialist, they also frequently transcend the essentialist clichés that dog his more academic pronouncements. And with a final, unexpected upward leap, Wonder Woman elevates Marston's putatively scientifically grounded musings about dominance and submission into the idealist domain of metaphysics and theology.

7

Although described in relentlessly secular terms in his psychological writings, Marston's lifelong effort to valorize erotic submission started to take on a more spiritual dimension when reframed in terms of a fantasy about an Amazon superhero. This spirituality may not have been obvious to Marston himself, at least at first, for he was clearly not a conventionally religious man. Like many intellectuals of his generation, he seems to have imagined that the most compelling explanations and solutions for the state of the world were to be found in the doctrines of an essentially materialist biology; and he attempted to strengthen his own academic discipline of psychology by grafting it onto those branches of inquiry.

Nevertheless, the need to defend his *Wonder Woman* comics from Josette Frank's concerns about their general unsuitability for children jolted him into thinking in more theological terms. This is most clearly apparent in a five-page letter Marston wrote to W. W. D. Sones, a Professor of Education at the University of Pittsburgh, and another member of M. C. Gaines's advisory committee. Gaines seems to have drawn Sones into the conflict between Marston and Frank, as a kind of "tie-breaker." Pleading his case to Sones, Marston repeated many arguments that he had made first in *The Emotions of Normal People*, but he also made the following claims:

> Wonder Woman breaks the bonds of those who are slaves to evil masters. But she doesn't leave the freed ones to assert their own egos in uncontrolled self-gratification. Wonder Woman binds the victims again in *love chains*—that is, she makes them submit to a *loving* superior, a beneficent mistress or master, who in every case represents "God," or Goodness, or Aphrodite, Godess [sic] of Love and Beauty. Freedom usually goes through a stage, as in progressive education, where it becomes detrimental through lack of discipline.

Marston's scare-quotes around the word "God" suggest that he did not wish to be understood too literally—that his work on Wonder Woman was not to be equated with, say, Christian proselytizing. They also suggest something of his own discomfort at finding himself employing such a suspiciously irrational concept. But the basic implication is clear; the complex notion of submission that Marston has been trying to portray through his depictions of bondage play in his comics is an entirely familiar spiritual paradox. It is a form of submission-as-liberation, a freedom-in-chains, that can only come from surrender to the loving authority of divinity.

It's worth noting how very different Marston's account of the relationship between the sacred and the sexual is from the more academically fashionable theories of his early twentieth-century contemporary, Georges Bataille. For Bataille, religious ecstasy and sexual pleasure unite in the experience of violent self-shattering—a *jouissance* or excess of pleasure-as-pain. But for Marston, the erotic logic of dominance and submission does not lead to theology conceived as a form of excess, but something like the opposite: a divine restraint. What he seeks to convey through Wonder Woman's "love chains" is, quite literally, the pleasurable "discipline" of (self) limitation. When he insists further to Sones that, "giving to others, being controlled by them, submitting to other people cannot possibly be enjoyable without a strong erotic element," the argument is not so much that we learn to give pleasure in being taken but rather that we learn to take pleasure in giving.

In a theological context, the position that it is better to give than receive is of course entirely familiar; so familiar that we can all too easily nod in assent to it without really thinking about what is being said. But the implications of this position, as spelled out in both the words and the Passion of Christ, are far less readily assented to-even by many who call themselves "Christians." It is better to give than receive also means that is better to serve than to rule, better to surrender than to fight, better to obey than command, and better to submit than to dominate. It is the most difficult, most radical version of this notion that Marston echoes in what is also one of the most often repeated phrases of his *Wonder Woman* stories: "The only real happiness for anybody is to be found in the obedience to loving authority."[65] Marston placed exactly these words in the mouth of Hippolyta as the closing line of his very last story, written when he knew he was dying of cancer. They consequently stand as a kind of *reductio* of Wonder Woman's philosophy, and their homiletic ring is surely unmistakable. But the point of interest to theologians, scholars of sexuality, and comic book historians alike may be less that Marston finally advocated a fairly conventional religious philosophy, but that he arrived there by such putatively secular and even transgressive means.

The fact that Marston's fascination with gender, sexuality, and the fantasy of a female superhero led him to an essentially sacred understanding of submission as "obedience to loving authority" casts an interesting light on some contemporary theological debates about the nature—and the very possibility—of a specifically *feminist* Christianity. As Sarah Coakley has observed in the opening pages of her important work of feminist theology, *Powers and Submissions*, the dominant secular intellectual paradigms of the past few hundred years do not valorize submission:

> The Enlightenment demand for an empowered human "autonomy," despite all the intellectual criticism it has accrued in recent philosophical debate, has in practice barely been softened by postmodernity's more nebulous quest for the state of "agency," and its implicit adulation of infinite consumer choice. In neither case— that of "autonomy" or "agency"—is any concomitant form of human "submission" an obvious asset.[66]

However, and by contrast, in the realm of Christian theology, "the most influential conglomerate of 'neo-orthodox' and 'post-liberal' (male) theologians" of recent decades has tended to focus upon Christ's vulnerability—his embrace of human weakness and self-exposure to human cruelty—with the somewhat paradoxical result that submission "has become . . . identified with divine 'power'."[67] As Coakley notes, some feminist theologians have questioned this "adulation of vulnerability," on the grounds that such a strategy "reinstantiates, in legitimated doctrinal form, the sexual, physical, and emotional abuse that feminism seeks to expose." At its most blunt, their argument is that "an abused God merely legitimate abuse."[68]

For Coakley, this question of whether we should or should not valorize submission "cuts to the heart of what separates Christian and post-Christian feminism," and leads her to explore the problem in a brilliant essay on the meanings of Christ's *kenōsis*—that is, on the Godhead's "self-emptying" act of fleshly incarnation "in the likeness of a man." She first outlines a disagreement between Rosemary Radford Reuther and Daphne Hampson on the value of *kenōsis* as a concept within feminist theology. Reuther asserts that Christ's self-sacrificing vulnerability is a rebuke of patriarchal assumptions; but Hampson sharply responds that while *kenōsis* "may well be a model which men need to appropriate, and which may helpfully be built into the male understanding of God . . . for women, *the theme of self-emptying and self-abnegation is far from helpful as a paradigm.*" In other words (and in what I hope readers will immediately recognize is a close cousin of one of Marston's basic assumptions), while men might need to learn the value of submission, the opposite may be true for women.[69]

Coakley is fully sympathetic to Hampson's concerns; she recognizes the historical fact that patriarchal Christian males have often valorized doctrines of submission to reinforce oppression on the basis of gender, and that this makes it a particularly problematic theological concept for many women. Coakley is nevertheless troubled by the possibility that Hampson may be throwing out the spiritual baby with the bathwater of discrimination, as it were. For Coakley, the concept of submission—at least, when reconfigured as a special form of "self-effacement"—turns out to be spiritually essential. Indeed, it is so fundamental to her approach to divinity that to abandon it would be give up the field entirely: "if I could not make spiritual and theological sense of this *special* form of power-in-vulnerability," she declares, "I would see little point in continuing the tortured battle to bring feminism and Christianity together."[70]

What does Coakley mean by "self-effacement" in this highly specialized sense? In one of the most passionately written passages of *Powers and Submissions*, she describes it as nothing more or less than a "silent waiting on the divine in prayer" in which we " 'make space' for God to be God."

> Such prayer may use a repeated phrase to ward off distractions, or be wholly silent; it may be simple Quaker attentiveness, or take a charismatic expression (such as the use of quiet, rhythmic "tongues"). What is sure, however, is that engaging in any such regular and repeated "waiting on the divine" will involve great personal commitment and (apparently) great personal risk; to put it in psychological terms, the dangers of a too-sudden uprush of material from the unconscious, too immediate a contact of the thus disarmed self with God, are not inconsiderable. . . . But whilst risky, this practice is profoundly transformative, "empowering" in a mysterious "Christic" sense; for it is a feature of the special "self-effacement" of this gentle space-making—this yielding to a divine power which is no worldly power—that it mark one's willed engagement in the pattern of cross and resurrection, one's deeper rooting and grafting into the "body of Christ." "Have this mind in you," wrote Paul, "which was also in Christ Jesus."[71]

Admirable in its refusal to adopt an elitist attitude toward the various forms of prayer, and unblinking in its assessment of the genuine risks of introspective spiritual practice, this account of Christian "self-effacement" might seem at first to be miles away from the more "worldly" sense of erotic submission explored in Marston's *Wonder Woman* stories. And in fact, Coakley has already explicitly dismissed erotic submission in the very first sentence of her book; acknowledging that it is only in "the titillating form of sexual bondage" that submission is currently "in vogue," she regards it as self-evidently irrelevant to her theological and ethical concerns.[72]

But can the sexual be so swiftly and peremptorily separated from the sacred? Can the attempt to "make space" for God through, for example, "the use of quiet, rhythmic 'tongues'" be so easily distinguished from an erotically attained dissolution of the self? And do the risks and pains that attend upon rigorous spiritual inquiry really bear so little resemblance to sadomasochistic practice that we can declare the difference always and self-evidently apparent? (I cannot resist pointing out that Coakley herself describes the project of aligning feminism with Christianity as "tortured.") There are no easy responses to these questions, of course. But they derive what force they have from the fact that the mutual imbrication of sexual and spiritual energy is everywhere apparent throughout the history of religion in the West, and perhaps throughout the world, if one is willing to look for it—as Coakley no doubt knows.[73] Within the Judeo-Christian tradition alone, the metaphorical interchangeability of sexual and spiritual desire was established at least as far back as the "Song of Songs"; and the historical transformations in our understanding of the vexed relationship between these two categories of profound yearning—particularly from the medieval period through the Renaissance and into modernity—is a subject worthy of several books.

Having entered this territory, it is impossible for me to do more than gesture toward the inexhaustible complexity of the issues involved. But I make this gesture, however inadequate it may seem, because I think we require reminding of this complex history, and of the conceptual and political challenges we face when we choose to celebrate *or* repudiate submission—whether in erotic *or* spiritual terms. We need to acknowledge the longstanding tendency for the sexual and the sacred to become confused, even as we note the perhaps equally longstanding desire to tear them apart, sometimes by violence.

8

William Marston's *Wonder Woman* comics can therefore help us to see a possibility that Coakley overlooks. They can help us to recognize that the effort to valorize the spiritual concept of submission from a feminist perspective is neither opposed to nor divorced from the effort to theorize the experience of erotic bondage from a similarly feminist perspective. Thus, where Coakley's arguments begin from the assumption that erotic bondage is at best irrelevant to a careful consideration of the meanings of spiritual submission, Marston's end with the discovery that the each of these things can be just like the other. For Marston's Wonder Woman, sex can be sacramental—bondage can be sacramental—because, in the words of John Donne, who also often refused the distinction between sexuality and spirituality, "to enter in these bonds is to be free."[74] Perhaps no other superhero invites us to consider this possibility.

Few of Wonder Woman's modern writers have been willing to explore this territory either—despite the fact that superhero comic books have supposedly become more "adult" and "sophisticated" in the last couple of decades.[75] This is hardly surprising, however. Marston's attempt to articulate a paradoxical doctrine of human liberation through a spiritualized "erotics of service" in the unlikely genre and medium of superhero comics was not straightforwardly legible in the 1940s; but in the present era, such a project is so baffling as to border on the unintelligible. Part of the problem is that we "postmoderns" seem no more capable than the average "modern" of framing divine love in erotic terms, except in the context of deliberately transgressive art and theory that—in an essentially post-Freudian way—tends to regard spiritual desire as a distorted expression of primary sexual instincts (witness the aforementioned Battaile).[76] In fact, Marston himself probably thought of the relationship between the sexual and the spiritual in those terms, granting sexuality a biological "reality" that he could not bestow upon the spiritual. But he combined this belief in the primacy of sex with an equally strong commitment to a vision of social progress through sexual liberation. Consequently, his conception of the power of erotic love is so positive that it does not seem to strike him as particularly transgressive to render it in divine terms—but merely as appropriate. This remarkable faith-in-sex might be seen as basic to all of Marston's thinking, and it is also perhaps the least fashionable of his ideas—likely to strike many orthodox people of faith as an idolatrous blasphemy, but also likely to be dismissed as hopelessly naïve by post-Foucauldian theorists of sexuality, who have learned to regard any theory of liberation-through-Eros with skepticism.

Falling between Freud and Foucault as he does, then, Marston inevitably suffers by comparison with either. His theories probably could not be more out of place in modern intellectual culture. But nevertheless, his effort to give them form through the adventures of an Amazon superhero resulted in the creation of a fantasy world wherein traditional oppositions between the secular and the sacred, sex and spirituality, and submission and dominance are undone. This not only makes Marston's Wonder Woman a potential site of political resistance, and an unexpected place from which to examine some of the challenges presented by feminism to theology, but also one of the most exciting points from which to interrogate the assumptions of the superhero genre about such key concepts as sex, gender, power, and religion. In a genre where women still figure most prominently as maternal caregivers, as clueless lovers who mistakenly attempt to impose the conventions of domesticity on the hero, as hostages, and as femme fatales, Diana stands out as a glorious exception who perhaps even now has yet to reach her full potential. Of all the superheroes I write about in this book, I regard Wonder Woman as the one about whom the most could still be said—the one with the greatest potential both creatively and critically.

For me, the critical work, at least, can begin with a recognition of the deconstructive energies that Marston bequeathed to us when he moved from psychological theory to comic book fantasy, and invented the world of Wonder Woman. Perhaps now, the list of contradictions and ironies with which I began can be seen as positive rather than negative—as a refusal of some of the most limiting binary oppositions of our culture. For Wonder Woman is a fantasy figure who asserts, against the entire masculinist symbolic order, that it is possible to be both beautiful *and* strong, to be nurturing *and* independent, to be emotional *and* intelligent, to be assertive *and* kind. Nor are these the only oppositions that she refuses: she comes from an artistically and technologically advanced culture, but insists that it is nevertheless possible to learn from nature; she espouses spiritual values but eschews fanaticism, dogma, and intolerance; she understands the arts of war, but teaches the lessons of peace. Her decline in popularity since her peak under Marston's stewardship may therefore not be a sign of our progress with regard to issues of gender and power since the 1940s, but just the opposite. Nevertheless, to the extent that all revolutions begin in the head—as fantasies, imagined possibilities of better ways of living and being—it is surely possible that, in the right creative hands, Wonder Woman could once again become a vital fantasy figure for men and women alike.

CHAPTER THREE

SPIDER-MAN: HEROIC FAILURE
AND SPIRITUAL TRIUMPH

1

Spider-Man's origin, as told in the near-perfect 11-page story from *Amazing Fantasy* #15 (August, 1962), departs from the standard formula of all prior superhero beginnings. Upon gaining their abilities, most first-generation or Golden Age comic book superheroes say something like: "powers such as these must be used for the good of mankind." By contrast Spider-Man, a second-generation or Silver Age superhero, says: "From now on I just look out for number one— that means—me!" Instead of discovering an altruistic agenda, he is discovered by an agent. Instead of pursuing thieves and killers in the underworld, he pursues fortune and celebrity in the showbiz world. He imagines that his new gifts set him apart from the concerns of ordinary humanity, with the exception of his loving guardians, Aunt May and Uncle Ben; he declares that he will "see to it that they're always happy, but the rest of the world can go hang."[1]

Thus, Peter Parker's most important transformation does *not* occur when he is bitten by that notorious "radioactive spider," thereby becoming strong, agile, and able to climb walls and ceilings. It occurs seven pages later, when he discovers that his Uncle Ben has been murdered—and that he could have prevented the crime but failed to act due to his own self-involvement. Only in his grief for Ben does he awaken to a painful recognition of human interdependence, learning in the harshest possible way that we cannot choose to stand apart from one another; and only in his guilt over his prior behavior does he belatedly realize that "with great power there must also come great responsibility."

Variants on this statement—probably the most famous final clause in comic book history—can be found in a range of more "respectable" sources, from the medieval-era writings of Christine de Pisan to the modern wartime speeches of Franklin Delano Roosevelt. Stan Lee himself, however, cites the influence of the Bible—specifically Luke 12:48: "For unto whomsoever much is given, of him shall be much required."[2] And in fact, beneath its secular surface, the impeccably crafted morality tale that is Spider-Man's origin story explores several familiar themes of Judeo-Christian theology, including the temptation of pride, the indelible and yet transformative experience of personal guilt, and the traumatic nature of revelation. But it is the problem of how one should understand God's "requirement," figured as the question of what, precisely, constitutes Spider-Man's heroic "responsibility," that most haunts the character in subsequent years.

What should I do with the gift I have been given? How should I live this life that is mine alone? These essentially spiritual questions are an urgent focus for all of Stan Lee's tenure on *The Amazing Spider-Man* comic book, and for several years after his departure. They manifest most obviously in the form of a compulsively reiterated plot structure in which Peter Parker renounces his heroic identity as Spider-Man, only to find himself compelled to take it up once more. In this chapter, I read this frequently repeated plot first in terms of psychoanalytic theories of trauma, as the symptomatic return of a repressed insight—the painful realization that no amount of earthly power could entirely mitigate human suffering or prevent injustice. I show how this repressed insight finally surfaces in Peter's encounter with yet another violent trauma, the death of Gwen Stacy (a famous story that I consider in close detail). I then draw a parallel between Peter Parker's "working through" of these traumas and a central message of Søren Kierkegaard's theological philosophy, in which spiritual (self) knowledge is said to emerge only from the suspension or failure of conventional ethics. In the process, I demonstrate that these repetitious experiences of heroic failure finally distinguish Spider-Man from all his fellows within the superhero genre, in psychological, spiritual, and heroic terms. Finally, I raise some disturbing questions about the sacrificial function of the innocent woman within this heroic and spiritual learning curve.

My purpose is not simply to render these intellectual concepts more accessible by applying them to a well-known figure of pop culture, a project that by itself runs the risk of patronizing popular art and popular audiences. I also hope to show that the comics themselves constitute a sophisticated approach to some profound problems of human agency in the face of suffering. Thus, the point of what follows is not just that psychoanalytic and existential philosophy can illuminate some key aspects of *The Amazing Spider-Man*, but also that *The Amazing Spider-Man* can in turn illuminate some key aspects of psychoanalytic and existential philosophy.[3]

2

Traumatic loss, guilt, and compensatory reaction are central aspects of Peter Parker's psychology from the outset of his career as a costumed adventurer, and his self-image is profoundly marked by the experience. As any longtime reader of the comics will know, he is more given to expressions of depressive self-loathing than any other superhero. Intriguingly, however, when he is actively engaged in his compensatory activities as Spider-Man—fighting super-villains or foiling muggers and bank-robbers—he becomes humorous, playful, and light-hearted, almost as if he is playing a game. How might this contradiction be explained?

Freud's investigations into the human response to trauma in *Beyond the Pleasure Principle* suggest that the concept of the game actually provides the necessary insight into Peter's behavior. Watching his grandson throw a cotton reel out of his playpen, retrieve it, and then throw it away again, Freud speculated that this repetitious activity—the "fort/da" [gone/there] game, as he named it—represented the child's attempt to soothe the anxiety he felt when left alone by his mother. Wondering why the game should prove pleasurable, when the experience of "losing" the mother was obviously traumatic, Freud suggested that while "[a]t the outset [the child] was in a *passive* situation . . . by repeating it [the mother's loss], unpleasurable though it was, as a game, he took on an *active* part. These efforts might be put down to an instinct for mastery that was acting independently of whether the memory was in itself pleasurable or not."[4] Peter's playfulness during his adventures as Spider-Man is therefore, in Freudian terms, entirely of a piece with his effort to master the trauma of Uncle Ben's loss.[5]

But Freud's further meditations on the relationship between anxiety and repetition suggest that this "instinct for mastery" in the face of traumatic events is rarely fully conscious, and often has a compulsive component. A seriously traumatized person, he says, will feel "obliged to *repeat* . . . repressed material as a contemporary experience instead of . . . *remembering* it as something belonging to the past."[6] Consequently, while some events may be too traumatic for a person to face directly, the "repressed" memory is never entirely forgotten. Instead, it returns in the symptomatic form of an obsessive thought or activity, a repetitive "acting out". Freud explains these repetitive symptoms as doomed attempts at self-soothing— doomed because, of necessity, they do not directly acknowledge the depth and extent of the original trauma, for all that they may provide some temporary relief from the psychic pain associated with it. (More problematically, such repetitious attempts at self-soothing may actually lead to further trauma—for example, when an abused child repeats the experience of his/her upbringing by seeking out an abusive partner.) Treatment therefore involves "working through" the repressed experience, in order to arrive at a more complete understanding of the past. The main barrier to the treatment, obviously, is that it requires that the patient give up the short-term benefits of the repetition-compulsion, and confront events that he or she has repressed due to their unbearable nature.[7]

At first, it might seem that this more elaborate account of the psychodynamics of trauma does not apply to Spider-Man. After all, Peter does not repress the knowledge of Ben's loss, but rather seems fully conscious of the role it plays in driving his actions as a superhero. In later flashbacks retelling his origin story, Peter is even depicted at the graveside of his dead guardian, swearing a vow to "never again refuse to use my spider power whenever it can help the cause of justice," and to spend the rest of his life "making up for the death of Uncle Ben."[8] But significantly, *no such scene occurs in the original story*. The flashbacks thus project onto the beginning of the *Spider-Man* series something that is actually conspicuously absent in the initial telling; and in the process, they simplify the emotionally complex reaction to Uncle Ben's death that Peter actually undergoes in Stan Lee and Steve Ditko's groundbreaking work on the character. Above all, they gloss over the deep ambivalence Peter expresses with regard to both the heroic role and his own suitability for it.

For example, in *The Amazing Spider-Man* #1, when Peter first dons his costume after Uncle Ben's death, he is not heading out to stop a crime, but is still trying to exploit his powers for their entertainment value—the difference being that he is now motivated by the practical need to raise money to take care of his Aunt May, rather than by his own adolescent hunger for adulation. It is only when a scaremongering journalist named J. Jonah Jameson starts to editorialize against him as a "bad influence on our youngsters" (in a satirical echo of the real-life anti-comics crusades of the prior decade) that Peter finally renounces his dream of a show-business career. When he does engage in heroic activity, saving Jameson's astronaut son from a faulty space-rocket, his actions are misinterpreted—he is accused of trying to cause the very disaster that he averts. "Everything I do as Spider-Man seems to turn out wrong!" he complains, wondering, "What good is my fantastic power if I cannot use it??" He even contemplates becoming the "menace" he is taken to be. "Perhaps," he thinks, "that is the only course left for me."[9]

Of course, Peter resists this temptation to use his powers for evil; but during his moments of introspection he remains unclear about their value and purpose, and generally ambivalent about the entire heroic project. For example, in *The Amazing Spider-Man* #3, he suffers a defeat at the hands—or more exactly the multiple mechanical arms—of Dr. Octopus, and promptly quits the role of superhero altogether. ("I'm a failure!" he declares, "Spider-Man is a joke . . . a nothing!") He only returns to the fray when another superhero, The Human Torch of the Fantastic Four, visits his high school and delivers a rousing speech on the nature of courage. But the Torch's words don't stay with Peter for long; just one month later, in the final panel of *The Amazing Spider-Man* #4, we again find him in the grip of an existential crisis, his speech balloons filled with as many question marks as exclamation points. Even though he has just captured the villainous Sandman, he is unable to discern the point of his heroic activity: "Am I really some sort of crack-pot, wasting my time seeking fame and glory??" he wonders. "Am I more interested in the adventure of being Spider-Man than I am in helping people?? Why do I do it? Why don't I give the whole thing up?" These questions remain unanswered, even as he decides to go on: "And yet I can't [give up]! I must have been given this great power for a reason! No matter how difficult it is, I must remain Spider-Man! And I pray that some day the world will understand!"[10]

In fact, over the course of Spider-Man's first decade or so, this basic process of renunciation and return repeats itself with remarkable frequency, both within single issues and across longer story arcs.

It receives its most iconic treatment in *The Amazing Spider-Man* #50, in a story entitled "Spider-Man No More," with its memorable splash page showing the Spider-Man costume abandoned in a garbage can—an image emblematic enough to be recreated more than three decades later by Sam Raime in the second *Spider-Man* feature film. But as should now be apparent, Peter's love-hate relationship with his Spider-Man identity is in place from the very beginning of the series, and is subject to increasing elaboration with each reiteration. Stan Lee himself clearly saw the pattern as a distinguishing feature of his favorite creation, and made it the central theme of another significant "anniversary issue," *The Amazing Spider-Man* #100, an important story in the Spider-Man canon for many reasons, since it also marked Lee's final turn as regular writer on the title. The comic thus stands as both a "summing up" of the series so far, and a fond farewell to the character by his first writer.

In the opening pages, Peter again resolves to give up his Spider-Man identity and lead a normal life—or as he puts it, in starkly melodramatic terms: "In order for Peter Parker to really live—Spider-Man must die!" This time he takes the drastic measure of drinking a potion designed to remove his spider powers. The potion induces a hallucinogenic nightmare in which Spider-Man is forced to battle his greatest enemies one by one—The Vulture, The Lizard, The Green Goblin, Dr. Octopus, the Kingpin—all the while hearing a haunting voice— the "voice of a friend," he says, though he cannot quite recognize who—calling his name, over and over. As he battles his enemies, he reflects on the meaninglessness of his actions, and acknowledges that he doesn't know why he has lived his life this way: "All I do is fight, fight, but for what?" His enemies question his sanity, and he can only echo their assessment, descending into agonized despair. He pulls himself back from this brink, however, with the following words: "Maybe I have been a failure, but I've never been a quitter, and I won't be now. I won't!" The imagery reflects this resolve; he delivers knockout blows to the Kingpin with each reiteration of his determination to fight on.

Having defeated his last enemy he then discovers the source of the voice of the "friend" he has been hearing. It turns out to be the literally heavenly voice of a dead man, speaking from out of the sun at the Manhattan horizon. It belongs to Captain George Stacy, a recently deceased member of the supporting cast, deliberately developed as a surrogate for Peter's original lost paternal figure, Uncle Ben himself.

This "heavenly father" tells Peter that he must embrace his heroic identity, despite the suffering it has caused him: "You have tortured yourself by trying to live a normal life! But you cannot! You must accept that fact! You are Spider-Man! It is your blessing—and your curse—forever"[11] (see Fig. 3.1).

The thinly veiled religiosity of this episode barely requires explication, complete as it is with an almost George Herbert–like evocation

Figure 3.1 A heavenly voice tells Peter Parker to embrace his identity as Spider-Man in this dream/vision from *The Amazing Spider-Man* #100. © Marvel Comics.

of the "voice of the friend," a voice that then advocates radical self-acceptance as a form of surrender. But for now, the point I want to emphasize is that stories like this one should prevent us from reducing Spider-Man's heroic motivation to a single-minded vow to "make up" for the selfish neglect that led to Uncle Ben's death. *That* story is just the one that Peter sometimes tells himself, and he has perhaps by now told it so often that even his fans and creators are capable of repeating it unthinkingly. But if we actually read his adventures, we discover something quite different. Instead of a single graveside oath upheld with grim determination, *á la* Batman, we find a persistent pattern of wild oscillation between the poles of hope and despair—repetitious outpourings of self-loathing and shame that nevertheless circle back to equally repetitious and essentially ungrounded reaffirmations of his Spider-Man identity. Boiled down to its essence the dramatic structure is almost absurdist, recalling the paradoxical formula of Samuel Beckett's work: "I can't go on, I'll go on."[12]

To put it another way, if we look at what Peter is repeatedly made to *do* by his creators, rather than what he is sometimes made to *say*, then both his feelings of guilt and his crime-fighting can seem to have an obsessive-compulsive quality about them. His expressions of self-loathing and guilt with regard to Ben's death start to appear more neurotic than heroic. For example, his constant cry—"It's all my fault!"—simply doesn't stand up to close scrutiny. He didn't actually shoot his uncle, after all, a burglar did, and yet he seems compelled to take on more responsibility than belongs to him. He is getting something from all that delicious guilt. But the driven, compulsive nature of Peter's web-slinging is perhaps most apparent from his many failed attempts to renounce the behavior. Time and again, he comes to recognize that his heroic activities interfere with the normal functioning of his career and his interpersonal relationships. Time and again, he notes the irony that his perpetual do-gooding may actually be damaging him, and those he cares about. Time and again, he hits an emotional "bottom," and admits that his compensatory efforts to make up for Uncle Ben's loss have had destructive and harmful consequences. Time and again, he resolves to stop. But, like an alcoholic returning to the bottle, or more accurately, like a co-dependent, resentfully but perpetually riding to the rescue, he always finds himself donning his Spider-Man costume once again.

Some might be inclined to deflect the force of this analysis with the glib observation that if Peter gave up being Spider-Man, Marvel

Comics could no longer profit from his adventures. But this would be to miss the point. Bruce Wayne does not go through nearly as many bouts of agonized indecision in relation to his Batman identity, after all; nor does the Green Lantern constantly wonder whether the universe needs him to police it; Wonder Woman never seriously considers abandoning humanity and returning to Paradise Island; and so on. Only Spider-Man is so driven to renounce his heroic identity, and then to take it up again, in an endlessly repetitive cycle. And that cycle, I am suggesting, is inherent in the particular mechanisms of trauma and guilt that shape and drive his story. A deeper logic is at work here than can be explained by the profit motive of a large corporation, or even by the conscious intent of an individual writer: the unconscious logic of the traumatic wound. (I suspect that it is this logic, as much as any Romantic vision of art, that often underwrites the writer's familiar claim that some characters seem, in an almost uncanny and mysterious way, to "write themselves.")

Following Freud, the question that emerges from this analysis is "What is Peter Parker trying to avoid?" What repressed knowledge drives this symptomatically repetitive cycle of refused and reluctantly renewed heroism, a heroism that turns out to be only putatively motivated by guilt over Uncle Ben's death? What could be more profoundly traumatic than *that*? What could be *worse*? Unfortunately for Peter, it would take the radical failure of his chosen mode of self-soothing—a radical failure of his heroic activity—to bring this still more traumatic knowledge to the surface. That failure occurred in the early 1970s, more than 10 years after Spider-Man first appeared on the newsstands, in one of the most important stories in the comic book superhero canon: "The Night Gwen Stacy Died." But before describing the singular impact of that story, it is first necessary to say something about the unfortunate girl named in the title, and her special place in Peter's troubled life.

3

Gwen Stacy was introduced into the Spider-Man supporting cast in *Amazing Spider-Man* #31 (Dec. 1965), just as the run by the original creative team of Stan Lee and Steve Ditko was drawing to its end. At this stage, Lee and Ditko were experimenting with what remains an unusual narrative innovation in the genre, by allowing Peter Parker to age at a relatively normal rate.[13] Peter had just graduated from high school, and with #31 he enrolled at Empire State University, meeting both Gwen and another soon-to-be-significant supporting character, Harry Osborn, on his first day. Although Peter may have felt love before (for J. Jonah Jameson's long suffering secretary, Betty Brant), his initial encounter with Gwen is presented as part of a significant rite of passage: the movement from the relatively immature emotional world of the teenager to the supposedly deeper experiences of young adulthood.

Unable to decide whether she is irritated or fascinated by the bookish, self-absorbed Mr. Parker, Ditko's Gwen at first resembles another of Peter's early crushes, his high school friend Liz Allen. But Gwen is quickly established as having a quite different personality: smarter, more sophisticated, and even fiery. (For example, in #37, she slaps Peter when she thinks he is being fresh.) Her early exchanges with Peter are all tense and unfriendly, despite the curiosity she expresses about him in the privacy of her thought-balloons. Visually, Ditko's Gwen projects attractive confidence with a hint of cruelty. Strikingly, in all her appearances during Ditko's tenure, Gwen's outfits are colored bright red, while the barrettes in her hair give her an odd, devil-horned look; but the end result is more suggestive of haughty pride than seductive sensuality, thanks to Ditko's deceptively simple figure-drawing and deliberately flat line work.[14]

But when John Romita Sr. replaced Steve Ditko as the regular artist, with #39, everything changed. Romita had drawn superheroes before (he came to *Spider-Man* after a short stint on *Daredevil*), but as most comic book historians note, his more extensive background was in Romance comics. Consequently, under Romita's pencil, all the characters in the series received glamorous makeovers. The paradigmatically puny Peter Parker finally escaped from the imprisoning chrysalis of awkward adolescence. His outmoded 1950s wardrobe of dark blue suits and "young fogey" sweater-vests gradually gave way to blue jeans and far-out fringed shirts. Even his unfashionably short haircut started to look less utilitarian and more like a consciously "retro" choice (think Elvis Presley in his Hollywood years). But more immediate and obvious than Peter's visual change was that of the female characters. Ditko's conservatively styled and slightly standoffish women morphed almost overnight into impossibly hot chicks, newly dressed for the sexual revolution in floral blouses, miniskirts, and knee-high leather boots. No less significant than this change in the look of the comic was a change in attitudes. With Romita's arrival,

Peter's emotional world got warmer. In Romita's very first issue, Peter not only exchanged friendly words with Harry Osborn for the first time, and buried the hatchet with an old rival, Ned Leeds, but even his greatest personal nemesis, the bullying Flash Thompson, showed some signs of softening towards him. In fact, Peter would never again be as lonely and isolated as he was during his high school days.

Romita's most significant contribution to the Spider-Man universe came a few months later, however, in the final panel of #42—the first full appearance of a red-headed, slang-slinging bombshell named Mary Jane Watson. The artist's experience as the illustrator of teen-age romantic melodramas no doubt played a role in the subsequent characterization of Mary Jane as a classic feminine archetype (or stereotype, depending on your perspective): the "bad girl." Certainly, it is interesting to note that up until this point there were no obvious "good girls" or "bad girls" in *The Amazing Spider-Man* (Betty Brant, Lee and Ditko's most fully developed female character, was an intriguingly contradictory mixture of independence, practicality, impetuousness, and vulnerability—harder to pigeonhole, but also far too sensible to serve for long as a young superhero's love interest). But Romita's rendering of Mary Jane perfectly complemented Stan Lee's natural propensity for pop-operatic plots and pseudo-hipster dialogue. Sexy and sassy, but also flighty, unreliable, and at times downright bitchy, Mary Jane introduced a hitherto absent element of dangerous desire into Peter's life.[15]

Given the evermore soapy drift of these undercurrents, the arrival of a "bad girl" required the creation of a counterpart, and as the only other regular female member of the cast, the role of "good girl" fell upon Gwen. The modification of her personality to fit this new assignment was achieved in part by the introduction of her father, Police Captain George Stacy. While Mary Jane was left (for the time being) without parents or backstory, Gwen was increasingly portrayed as the concerned and dutiful daughter. Unfortunately, this meant that when either her father or Peter found themselves battling the criminal activities of super-villains like the Shocker, the Kingpin, and Dr. Octopus, Gwen's primary role was to weep, wail, and worry. This overall softening of her character was reinforced by Romita's drawings. Gwen's smart red outfits were retired, and her devil-horn barrettes replaced by a black hair band that gave her a more innocent schoolgirl look. Over the years, this simple visual device has become something of a fetish, in the most precise meaning of the term: a totemic object that both signifies and wards off potentially distressing knowledge. In flashback sequences, Gwen is never portrayed without that hair band, thereby effectively erasing Ditko's more emotionally volatile character from history, and ensuring that only "good girl Gwen" persists in the collective memory of comicdom.

The classic virgin/whore dichotomy was thus inserted into the Spider-Man myth in the form of a love triangle. Who would Peter pair off with, Gwen or Mary Jane? Under Stan Lee's direction, Peter fell for Gwen Stacy, and fell hard. His oscillating moods were now tied to the ups and downs of their relationship; he thought about her constantly as he went about his heroic business; he repeatedly agonized over whether to reveal his secret identity to her; and, in yet another variation on the pattern of renunciation and return, he even attempted to give up his powers to pursue a "normal" life with her (of course, this plan did not succeed). The pressure of maintaining his secret identity would lead to constant misunderstandings and problems, but also created the opportunity for joyful reconciliation sequences. For a while, the cycle was dramatically satisfying, and Stan Lee milked it for all it was worth throughout the late 1960s, and into the early 1970s. Inevitably, however, the situation too became repetitious, and the letter pages of the comic began to reflect reader dissatisfaction. The result was a developmental crisis for both the character and the creators. Perhaps not un-coincidentally, Stan Lee chose this moment to quit the comic he had steered for a decade, leaving the problem to be resolved by his successor, Gerry Conway.

Conway was just 19 years old. He had little more than a high school education, and an uneven track record at Marvel, having spent a couple of years writing less popular heroes like Daredevil, the Sub-Mariner, and Thor. From a contemporary perspective, the decision to hand Marvel's flagship property over to him is simply astonishing—it's impossible to imagine an equivalent decision being made today. But the company was not yet the corporation it would become. At the time, Conway was one of only four writers working at Marvel, including Stan Lee. Roy Thomas (the more senior and obvious choice) preferred writing team books like *The Avengers*, and encouraged Lee to give Conway the book; and Lee, apparently with some trepidation, agreed.[16]

As only the second regular writer to handle the character, Conway had a unique opportunity. Although obviously beholden to the work of his predecessors, he could take the established elements of the continuity in a genuinely new direction. To his everlasting credit, Gerry Conway seized the moment. In a bold stroke, he decided to resolve the problem of Lee's dangling love story by snipping the thread of Gwen Stacy's life, in *The Amazing Spider-Man* #121. Interestingly, he seems initially to have considered this radical move in fairly conservative terms, as part of a return to the overall mood of the original Lee/Ditko run, when Bad Things just happened to Peter an awful lot.[17] But inadvertently, his decision would not only cut to the core of Lee and Ditko's creation; it would violate the traditional generic conventions of the superhero genre itself.

4

Events are exquisitely paced throughout the comic book in question. For several tense pages, we are allowed to believe that Peter will save Gwen, in typical superhero fashion. Nevertheless, Peter's initial discovery that Gwen has been kidnapped by his arch enemy, the Green Goblin, is genuinely chilling; Spider-Man finds her handbag, abandoned amidst evidence of a struggle, with the Goblin's calling card, a small Halloween lantern, sitting nearby. "Oh my Lord," he whispers, his words rendered in reduced font in an oversize balloon by Artie Simek—even the style of the lettering is employed to convey the awful magnitude of the moment. There follows a page of desperate searching, as Spider-Man swings around Gil Kane and John Romita's lovingly detailed renditions of the New York skyline. Then, upon finding the Goblin atop one of the towers of the Brooklyn Bridge, with Gwen apparently unconscious beside him, the anticipated battle occurs. The fight sequence is penciled in Kane's characteristically dynamic manner, filled with foreshortened figures, bent and twisted in acrobatic poses, and includes a full half-page devoted to what, in a more conventional story, would have been Spider-Man's knockout punch.[18]

But the Green Goblin recovers to strike Gwen's body from the bridge with his bat-glider. In a dramatic panel stretching the full height of the comic page, we see her, high and tiny, plunging down to a watery grave. The next panel is smaller, a close up of Spider-Man on top of the bridge, firing his web-shooter to catch Gwen before she hits. "Did it!" he cries, snagging her leg, and, as he pulls her back toward him, he starts to babble in self-congratulatory relief: "Spiderpowers, I love you. Not only am I the most dashing hero on two legs— I'm easily the most versatile," and so on. Once again, the artistic team of Kane and Romita wonderfully augments Conway's bitterly ironic script. But as we turn to the next page, to find Spider-Man holding Gwen once more, the awful truth becomes apparent. The beautiful girl in his arms is dead.[19]

The precise cause of Gwen's death is at first obscure. Being hit by the Goblin's jet-powered glider alone might have been sufficient to cause fatal injury, although neither Spider-Man nor the Goblin consider that possibility. The Goblin himself declares: "A fall from that height would kill anyone before they hit the ground." But he is hardly a reliable witness. He might have killed Gwen "off-panel," before she fell (Spider-Man was never given a chance to examine her); and given his deranged mental state, even the Goblin himself might not know for sure. But then there is another possibility, suggested by a sound effect placed near Gwen's head in the panel depicting the moment where she is caught by Spider-Man's web. "SNAP!" It is a small sound effect, in marked contrast to more typical comic book noise indicators—unobtrusive enough to be missed on a first pass, particularly by an eager reader—and, according to Conway in later interviews, too quiet for Spider-Man to hear. Nevertheless, the clear but unstated implication is that Gwen's neck breaks when she is pulled up short by Spider-Man's web-line—meaning that Gwen Stacy may not have died in spite of Spider-Man's attempt to save her, but *as a result* (see Figure 3.2).

With this implication, the events of Gwen's death were rendered doubly traumatic, for besides the immediate blow of her loss was a second blow to Peter's self-understanding. As we have seen, his "official" motivation, following his failure to save Uncle Ben, is to spend the rest of his life preventing further suffering and injustice. But when Gwen dies, despite and perhaps even because of his best efforts, the relationship between guilt and responsibility central to Peter Parker's self-understanding is exposed as a self-protective fiction—keeping at bay the awareness that we live in an unpredictable universe where Bad Things happen that *no one* can prevent. Thus, Peter and his readers were forced to face the possibility that, in taking up the mantle of "hero," he had only replaced one self-serving fantasy (that his powers set him apart from involvement with ordinary humanity) with another (that his powers allow him always to save others from harm). With Gwen's death, the true cause of Peter's neurotic guilt over Ben's murder was inadvertently revealed. His exaggerated sense of responsibility served not only to compensate for Ben's loss, but also (and

Figure 3.2 The death of Gwen Stacy from *The Amazing Spider-Man* #121. Note the "SNAP!" sound effect, placed near Gwen's head. © Marvel Comics.

perhaps more important) to sustain a comforting illusion of safety and control in a profoundly uncertain world.

Paradoxically, then, given that the superhero genre by definition concerns the fantastic adventures of superpowered beings, the events of Gwen Stacy's death challenged both Peter Parker and his readership to accept the reality and consequences of human *powerlessness*. Indeed, by emphasizing the fundamental nature of human powerlessness as he did in this story, Gerry Conway also challenged the central fantasy of the generic form to which it belongs: the fantasy that superpowers present a viable solution to the reality of life's pains and problems. Thus, we arrive at the third and perhaps most painful aspect of Gwen Stacy's death, the reason that the comic transcends its own status as a representation of trauma to become that more rare aesthetic animal, a traumatic representation. For in the context of Spider-Man's official heroic history, "The Night Gwen Stacy Died" is an assault upon the traditional form of the superhero comic itself—a hitherto unprecedented act of self-reflexive violence.[20] It is for this reason, I believe, that *Amazing Spider-Man* #121 is often cited by comic book historians as marking an epochal division in the superhero genre, the passage from the joyful optimism of the so-called Silver Age to the more uncertain, pessimistic, and cynical Bronze Age.[21] The psychoanalytic understanding of trauma as a symptom of an individual's history is given a broader valence by this act of periodization, in which all subsequent superhero comics are understood as bearing unconscious witness to the impact of Gwen's death.

The traumatic consequences of this self-reflexive violence are further suggested by the reactions of comic creators and fans. In fact, within this community, the reaction to Gwen's death unfolded precisely according to Cathy Caruth's influential post-Freudian account of traumatic experience, when she declares that "the [traumatic] event is not assimilated or experienced fully at the time, but only belatedly, in its repeated possession of the one who experiences it."[22] To elaborate: the initial obfuscations around Gwen's cause of death (maybe it was the shock of the fall; maybe she was already dead; maybe Spider-Man inadvertently killed her) suggest that even for the creators, her loss was too much to experience fully at the time. To these obfuscations, we may add the fact that while Conway's script specifies that Gwen dies at the George Washington Bridge, Gil Kane's drawings are of the Brooklyn Bridge. Some might dismiss this inconsistency as a mere artist's error, but there can be no denying the consequences;

the location of the event was henceforth and forever marked by the kind of confusion associated with the traumatic disruption of memory. Usually, Peter Parker remembers Gwen being thrown off the Brooklyn Bridge, but *sometimes* he remembers it as the George Washington Bridge.

Gerry Conway's own narrative of the creative process is marked by a similar failure of memory; when asked in an interview by Tom DeFalco some years later whether "Gwen was still alive until her neck snapped" Conway answered:

> Honestly, I don't know—I'm not sure why I added that sound effect or what I meant to accomplish . . . it was the result of a sub-conscious decision. Consciously, I've always thought that she was already dead when Spider-Man caught her. But if that's true, why did I put that "SNAP" in? . . . It's one of the very few inspired moments in my career when my subconscious mind made a choice that meant so much more than my conscious mind ever intended. That said, I'd sure like to believe that she was already dead.[23]

Conway's reply is refreshingly ingenuous, but even as he emphasizes the "subconscious" aspect of his decision, he admits that the implications of the "SNAP!" sound effect remain almost too much for him to accept. (Conway is not the only one involved to have fuzzy memories around these events; although he was editor-in-chief of Marvel at the time, and Gwen's co-creator, Stan Lee claims not to recall being consulted about the decision to kill Gwen—although Conway and others assert that he was, and that he gave his reluctant approval.)

As further evidence of the belated assimilation of the trauma, we can point to the fact that four months would pass before Marvel directly addressed the confusion over Gwen's cause of death, in an editorial comment on the letters page of #125.

> . . . it saddens us to have to say that the whiplash effect she under-went when Spidey's webbing stopped her so suddenly was, in fact, what killed her. In short, it was impossible for Peter to save her. He couldn't have swung down in time; the action he did take resulted in her death; if he had done nothing she still would cer-tainly have perished. There was no way out. . . . We've said before that our stories just seem to write themselves, and that we often don't have any control over them. This was such a case . . . So don't

blame Gerry. Don't blame Stan. Don't blame anyone. Only the inscrutable, inexorable workings of circumstances are responsible this time.

Here, the traumatic facts are finally acknowledged, but the origins of the trauma remain mystified. Taken aback by the outpouring of pain and anger Gwen's death had inspired in the ranks of fandom, the creators present themselves as no less at the mercy of fate than Gwen herself—something that may be true at a philosophical level, but which with regard to this particular event is obviously a convenient fiction.[24] The lesson of Spider-Man up until this moment had always been "with great power must also come great responsibility." But Gwen Stacy's death was apparently too traumatic for even the most powerful people in Spider-Man's universe—his writers—to take responsibility for it.

5

And what of Spider-Man's own reaction? Well, initially, it seems as if he is simply going to take all the blame yet again, in yet another repetition of his reaction to the foundational loss of his career. Thus, we find him in the following issue, grieving over Gwen's body, when a sympathetic policeman approaches him to say that an ambulance has arrived. He responds that Gwen doesn't need an ambulance, because "she's dead—and Spider-Man killed her." The policeman has little option but to take these perhaps ill chosen words literally, and Spider-Man is forced to flee the scene having yet again been mistaken for a criminal. He then tracks down the Goblin, and although he is finally able to resist the temptation to take murderous revenge, the Goblin is accidentally killed as a result of his own evil machinations. Spider-Man finds no satisfaction in the death of his foe, but only more evidence of the random nature of existence: "When a man dies—even a man like the Goblin—it should mean something. It shouldn't just be an accident—a stupid, senseless accident." It seems at first, then, as if Peter is as trapped as ever in the familiar cycle of loss, guilt, and belatedly inadequate heroism that has dominated his adventuring life since his origin story more than 10 years previously.[25]

But two months later, in *The Amazing Spider-Man* #123, Gerry Conway gives Peter a brief but remarkable speech in which he appears to refuse the burden of guilt that he is normally so ready to take up.

"Everywhere I turn . . . something reminds me of Gwen," he admits, but "It's not like I feel guilty—I know I did everything I could to stop it [her death]. Maybe that's what they mean by maturity: knowing how much you can expect of yourself." As Conway is swift to clarify, however, this doesn't mean that Peter feels OK; it means that he feels awful in a whole new way. "I feel alone," he says. "More terribly alone than I have ever felt in my life. . . . All I can think is—I'm alone now."[26] Importantly, Peter's hitherto uncharacteristic refusal of inappropriate guilt is taken as evidence of psychological growth, even as it is made clear that this growth is accompanied—or signaled—by a concomitant increase in the quality of his despair. "Maturity," for this superhero, combines the knowledge of his limitations with the experience of profound isolation.

With his ethical commitment harshly exposed as grandiose in aspiration and inadequate to the reality of human suffering, Peter is again presented with the choice to abandon his heroic identity. Attacked (again) by J. Jonah Jameson in his newspaper, Peter imagines (again) becoming the criminal he is accused of being: "I'll show you a menace, Jameson—"I'll show you a 'threat to public safety'!" But when he arrives at Jameson's building, he finds his enemy already menaced by a super-villain, and (of course) he ends up intervening to defend his longtime tormentor. Even this act is a repetition, since it's not the first time that Spider-Man has rescued Jonah from the forces of darkness—but it's a repetition that manages to be at once inevitable, even entirely predictable, and at the same time, mysterious. "You know something, Jonah?" he remarks, "I'm not sure why I'm doing this." And from this first mystery comes a second: "And another thing," he asks, even as he battles the monster, "why am I suddenly in such a blasted good mood?"[27]

We have progressed at this point from a traumatically symptomatic structure of unconscious repetition to a more self-conscious process of repetition-with-difference. In psychoanalytic terms, Peter might be said to have "worked through" some of his experience of loss. But another way of thinking about these events is provided by a more theological approach to the problem of repetition; the Kierkegaardian logic of repetition as a paradoxical structure that exposes the emptiness of human existence, while at the same time creating the conditions for a kind of spiritual advance, through it's very chastening effect.[28] The unfolding narrative of Peter Parker's emotional growth, from his first appearance in *Amazing Fantasy* #15 through to the death of Gwen Stacy and its aftermath, offers what I consider to be a striking parallel with Kierkegaard's account of spiritual progress as a three stage movement from the aesthetic via the ethical to the religious—a paradoxical "movement" that, as many commentators have pointed out, is itself a kind of repetition.[29]

According to Kierkegaard, the first of these attitudes—the aesthetic—is a default position, shared by all humankind, whether self-consciously or not. To adopt an aesthetic posture toward existence in Kierkegaard's terms is to seek the remedy for life's pains in the selfish pursuit of pleasure (a hedonism which can take both crude and elaborate forms—the pleasure of drunkenness and the pleasure of analyzing a literary text would both fall under this definition of the aesthetic). Clearly, Peter's attitude when he first receives his powers and devotes himself to the selfish pursuit of fame and fortune can be interpreted as that of an unsophisticated "aesthete." But with the death of Uncle Ben, his self-centered project of "looking out for number one" is vitiated; he cannot return to it without an awareness of all that it has cost him. He is left uncertain how to live, but with a profound and gnawing sense of anxiety regarding the "great responsibility" that has been imposed upon him. This anxiety parallels the important Kierkegaardian concept of "dread" exactly, in that it originates in Peter's growing awareness that morality may be fundamentally a matter of subjective choice—i.e., that the decision to use his powers responsibly rests with him and him alone (in Kierkegaardian terms, we might think of Peter's powers here as an allegory for the gift of subjective existence itself). Impelled by this anxiety, he confronts Kierkegaard's first Either/Or: the choice between the aesthetic and the ethical. As Kierkegaard writes (in the voice of his "ethical" surrogate author, Judge Wilhelm):

> My either/or does not in the first instance denote the choice between good and evil; it denotes the choice whereby one chooses good and evil/or excludes them . . . for the aesthetical is not evil, but neutrality . . . it is, therefore, not so much a question of choosing between willing the good or evil, as of choosing to will, but by this in turn the good and the evil are posited.[30]

The decision that Peter must make is therefore more basic than the adoption of a particular moral system. It is the decision to believe in the possibility of a moral system in the first instance: that is, to believe that there are such things as responsible and irresponsible actions (rather than just more or less pleasurable ones of a more or less sophisticated kind). The consequences of this basic decision are far reaching, for should one take it, *all future decisions become potentially objects of moral scrutiny*. To take the ethical choice is therefore to commit to a lifelong project; it is not a once-and-for-all decision to "do the right thing" so much as an endless process of self-examination and self-correction, with the possibility of failure constantly opening up before one like an abyss.

The fact that Peter has taken an essentially Kierkegaardian version of the ethical path is clear precisely because he does *not* express confident assurance in the virtue of his actions, but instead continually holds up his own heroic activity to critical scrutiny. The result, of course, is not liberation from the dreadful weight of his "great responsibility" but an intensification of that pressure. Thus, Peter's periodic abandonments of the heroic role become more extreme as his despair over his ability to live up to it grows. As we have seen, the culmination of this process, under Stan Lee's direction, is the classic story of *The Amazing Spider-Man* #100, which ends with a sequence in which a heavenly voice tells Peter that he must accept that he is Spider-Man; that is, his heroic identity expresses the essential truth of his being, and that his attempts to evade that truth are the cause of his suffering. This in itself is a Kierkegaardian response to the problem of suffering, in which Peter is essentially told that the only way one escapes existential despair is to become "willing to be the self which one truly is."[31]

However, with the death of Gwen Stacy, Peter encounters a repetition of the situation that prompted his initial ethical choice—the death of a loved one—with the crucial difference that this time there is nothing he could have done to prevent it; on the contrary, the actions he takes to prevent the tragedy cause it. With this event, then, conventional ethics founders on the rock of existential absurdity.[32] Spider-Man is confronted with the complete failure of the heroic role. Forced to acknowledge the limits of even his considerable power, he is left more profoundly isolated, "more terribly alone," than ever before. In the face of this "mature" despair, his decision to return yet again to the role of hero is marked as incomprehensible, even to him. Undertaking to protect a man who despises him, in a thankless effort to live according to a general principle of heroic self-sacrifice, the real-world value of which cannot be demonstrated, he remarks:

"I don't know why I am doing this." And yet, equally mysteriously, in the midst of this action, he finds he is in "a blasted good mood."

Is it too heavy-handed an imposition of religious terminology onto a supposedly secular popular adventure series to say that Spider-Man here commits a religious act when—against all experience, against reason, against his own will—he intervenes to protect J. Jonan Jameson from a werewolf, at the risk of his own life? Is it too much to interpret his "blasted good mood" as a kind of holy joy or even a sign of grace, bestowed upon him when in full awareness of the irony of the situation he nevertheless observes the (absurd) injunction to love his enemy? For some readers this may indeed be going too far. But I nevertheless find in Spider-Man's response to the greatest tragedy of his career an intriguing parallel with Kierkegaard's most famous and troubling claim; that is, the claim that a world of difference separates the notion of an ethical commitment from a genuinely religious one—and that this difference is rendered most palpable in the human encounter with life's absurdity.

What was Kierkegaard doing when he contrasted the genuinely religious with the merely ethical? Above all, he was motivated by his sense that the discourse of ethics had become far too reasonable, far too comfortably rational, after the Enlightenment philosophizing of Kant and Hegel, to be adequate to the demands of Christianity— demands that he saw as patently offensive to human reason, if taken seriously. Notoriously, Kierkegaard's example of true religious commitment is that of Abraham, who, in his willingness to sacrifice his son Isaac commits himself to what Kierkegaard called "a teleological suspension of the ethical." Insisting that we think of the story of Abraham and Isaac as a story of men of flesh and blood, bound by the most basic filial bond—rather than as a mythical allegory, say, about the importance of loving God over earthly things—Kierkegaard looked upon Abraham with stunned horror, as a potential murderer, or as insane: "humanly speaking, he is mad and cannot make himself intelligible to anyone."[33] And yet, Kierkegaard recognizes, it is in this very insanity that Abraham decisively establishes his relationship with God.

Kierkegaard's argument was designed to push his readers to recognize that Christianity cannot be itself when it accepts the terms of human reason. The awe-inspiring, shattering encounter with the more-than-human essence of the Almighty cannot be conveyed in rational terms, but is only available as a subjective experience of revelation, "self-enclosed and unintelligible," as Alisdair MacIntyre puts it, to anyone outside of that experience. As MacIntyre has also noted, "Theologians who recognize this have sometimes been dismayed by Kierkegaard's candor."[34] But Kierkegaard would have welcomed these expressions of dismay, because his purpose was to restore to Christianity what he saw as its originally scandalous character, "when it took the courage to face the lions to call oneself a Christian."[35] Merely saying you are a Christian doesn't make you one; it is only in your response to the call of God that you prove (or fail to prove) your faith. And according to Kierkegaard, it should be easy to see just by looking around that most of us are not answering God's call, at least as expressed by Christ in the New Testament. Being Christian, it turns out, is very hard to do.

In the putatively secular context of comic book superheroics, Spider-Man's adventures teach the same lesson with regard to the role of the hero. What Peter and his readers learn, through Spider-Man's traumatic, repetitious "progress," is that it is as hard to be a true hero as it is to be a true Christian, in Kierkegaard's terms—and for something like the same reasons. Despairing and despised, facing loss upon loss, Peter is never granted any objective proof or external evidence that he has chosen the righteous path, but is instead repeatedly thrown back upon the experience of subjective faith—in the form of a literal reaffirmation of his identity as Spider-Man—as the only truth. Most others regard his behavior as criminal and irrational; Peter himself fears that he is crazy. But he nevertheless persists, even in the face of the charges of criminality and irrationality. He persists, even in the face of his own inability to prevent the death of the innocents he would protect. And it is his persistence in the face of spectacular heroic failure, in the encounter with his all-too-human limitation, that makes him more than a hero, and perhaps closer to a saint.[36] In other words, although his repeated experiences of heroic failure may be symptomatic reiterations of his traumatic origin, they also turn out to be the necessary condition for his ultimately spiritual triumph. It is for this reason that Spider-Man can be described with surprising accuracy in the same paradoxical language of praise that Kierkegaard bestows upon Abraham, as both a "knight of infinite resignation" and a "knight of faith." In Kierkegaard's terms, in fact, Spider-Man might even be the greatest superhero of all: "great by that power whose strength is powerlessness, great by that wisdom whose secret is folly, great by that hope whose form is madness, great by that love which is hatred of oneself."[37]

6

At the risk of some reduction, we might say that while the psycho-analytic account of trauma posits a diagnosis and potential solution to human suffering, and while the existential philosophy of Kierkegaard posits another, *The Amazing Spider-Man* comic book series weaves both discourses together—and in this weaving, it resembles more than a few great works of twentieth-century art. I do not claim that the creators of the series always did this self-consciously, but this does not make Stan Lee, Steve Ditko, John Romita, Gerry Conway, or Gil Kane naïve or unsophisticated in their approach to issues of suffering, injustice, the limits of (super) human power, and the demands of responsibility. On the contrary, these great comic book writers and artists clearly marshaled the full resources of the superhero genre in their work on *Spider-Man*, and extended the traditional limits of that genre as they explored their chosen themes.

Nevertheless, the symbolic weight attached to the figure of the sacrificed woman within this larger narrative of heroic failure and spiritual triumph might give some feminist critics pause. In an important investigation of the representation of violence against women in Western art, Elisabeth Bronfen has argued that the symbolic power of the female victim resides in her capacity to speak the unspeakable: "Over representations of the dead feminine body, culture can repress and articulate its unconscious knowledge of death which it fails to foreclose even as it cannot express it directly."[38] More bluntly, we might say that in both popular and elite artworks, misogyny can be the preferred means to a nihilistic end. The young, innocent, female victim is thus the recurring centerpiece of stories that would make an otherwise intolerable claim: that the ultimate price of life is undeserved suffering, misery, and death. Gwen Stacy is to this extent one of a long line of dead girls, stretching back at least as far as Shakespeare's Cordelia—perhaps the archetypal innocent victim of English canonical literature—and frequently found today in our very darkest works of popular cinema, such as Marion Crane in Alfred Hitchcock's *Psycho*, or Tracy Mills in David Fincher's *Se7en*. Works of art that project this searing vision of existential suffering over the dead bodies of beautiful young women tend to be more than merely controversial. If they succeed, they traumatize their audiences. Indeed, the traumatic effect of Cordelia's death is well attested in the critical literature on Shakespeare, and is most vividly apparent in Nahum Tate's notorious rewrite of the play with a happy ending in which Cordelia survives—a version preferred by audiences over Shakespeare's original for more than a century.

The evidence suggests that Gwen's death struck comic book audiences no less painfully. According to several contemporary theorists, to be traumatized is to be haunted or even possessed. For example, as Thomas Pfau notes in a commentary on Freud, "an enigmatic past continues to trace the conscious history of . . . [the traumatized] subject with an oblique insistence for which 'haunting' seems just the right word."[39] In a similar vein, Cathy Caruth states that, "to be traumatized is precisely to be possessed by an image or event."[40] If these statements are correct, then Gwen Stacy's death is the single most traumatic event in superhero history, outweighing not only the death of Uncle Ben in Spider-Man's own story, but also the destruction of Krypton in Superman, and the death of Batman's parents.[41] Contemporary novelist Jonathan Lethem has described it as "the first romantic loss for a lot of guys my age," a statement quickly confirmed by a cursory trawl through the various comic-related blogs and discussion pages on the internet.[42] Today, almost 40 years after her demise, Gwen's superiority to Mary Jane Watson as a love-interest for Peter is still mooted in various online forums, while the details of her sexual history are debated with a remarkable intensity of feeling. Meanwhile, the sheer number of creators who have felt compelled to revisit the Peter/Gwen relationship attests to Gwen's haunting of the collective consciousness of comicdom; the list of names reads like a roll call of top industry talent, and includes Michael Allred, Brian Michael Bendis, Kurt Busiek, Peter David, Mike Deodato, Matt Fraction, Greg Larroca, Jeph Loeb, David Michelinie, Mark Millar, Peter Milligan, Alex Ross, Tim Sale, and J. Michael Straczynski.

However, perhaps no one has been more haunted by Gwen than her real killer, Gerry Conway. Nowadays a successful television writer and producer, Conway still finds himself fielding questions about Gwen's death. And back in 1975, apparently in response not only to reader demand but also to Stan Lee's request, Conway was the first Spider-Man writer to attempt some creative reparation for Gwen's loss. Of course, there was no persuasive way to bring the original

Gwen back; her death had been too decisively and publicly executed (so to speak). Therefore, Conway conceived the idea of returning her in the form of a clone, in *The Amazing Spider-Man* #142 (March, 1975). But this attempted restoration did not really produce the desired reparative result. Physically identical to Gwen, but without any memory of the last several months of her life, the Gwen-clone is a tragic figure, trapped in a world that no longer has a place for her. All she wants to do is resume what she imagines to be her former life, but the friends of the original Gwen, including Peter, recoil from this doppelgänger in horror and revulsion (the first sightings of the Gwen-clone by the various characters are particularly well handled by Conway and his penciler during this period, the brilliant and undervalued Ross Andru). Thus, like the parents who lose, regain, and again lose their child in W. W. Jacobs' classic gothic tale, "The Monkey's Paw," Peter, his readers, and perhaps even Gerry Conway and Stan Lee, all found themselves in the unpleasant position of wishing away the very thing they had so earnestly wished returned. The Gwen-clone is forced to acknowledge that the world has moved on since "her" death, and that she is not really wanted anymore. Understandably, she voluntarily departs the strip to start over elsewhere, after a moving final conversation with Peter, in #149 (also Conway's last issue of *The Amazing Spider-Man*).

This "original clone saga," as it has since become known, stands up remarkably well, although it is powerful precisely to the extent that it fails to do what it was presumably designed to do—that is, assuage the feelings of those who had been dismayed by Gwen's death. Instead, the Gwen-clone's brief and disruptive presence in Peter's world only confirms the ultimate impossibility of the real Gwen's restoration. Thus, just as Freud's account of compulsive repetition might lead us to expect, the story unconsciously repeats the very trauma that set it in motion. Perhaps sensing that he had not achieved his purpose with the Gwen-clone, Conway was driven to revisit these events (yet once more), over a decade later, during his tenure as the regular writer on *The Spectacular Spider-Man*, Marvel's companion comic to *The Amazing Spider-Man*. Here, Conway retroactively revised his clone story, revealing that clone-Gwen was actually a genetically modified woman named Joyce Delaney; in short, there was never really a Gwen-clone at all. The results were unsatisfactory, and created many loose ends that required further revision and rewriting. But despite making poor sense as a plot device, Conway's attempt to erase the Gwen-clone from the Spiderverse makes perfect sense as a further act of creative reparation for the secondary traumatic effects of his first clone saga.[43] It is as if, unable to undo Gwen's death, and the trauma that resulted from it, Conway was now attempting to undo his earlier attempt to undo Gwen's death, and the trauma that resulted from *that*.

Conway was perhaps lucky that his career as television writer took off when it did; otherwise he may well have been trapped in this vicious creative circle of traumatic repetition and reparation for many more years. For by this point, he was not the only writer working on Spider-Man (who was now appearing in four monthly comics on a regular basis), or the only writer haunted by Gwen. Before long, his attempt to undo the trauma of his Gwen-clone story would itself be undone by others, in yet another attempt to undo the original trauma of Gwen's loss! The cycle Conway had set in motion would thus continue to repeat itself without him, with increasingly negative consequences for the coherence of the storyline, well into the 1990s.[44]

Other subsequent attempts to master the trauma of Gwen's loss are still more repetitively symptomatic, and still less artistically satisfying; for example, so many different surrogates for Gwen have now been tossed from bridges and high buildings—this time to be saved by Peter—that such episodes have entirely lost the dramatic force they may once have had. (The device makes an appearance in a variant form in both the first and third of the *Spider-Man* movies, the first time with Mary Jane, and the second time with Gwen herself—even though the original trauma has never made it to the screen version of the story.) But a handful of creators have explored the Peter/Gwen relationship through dream sequences, flashbacks, and "alternative reality" scenarios, with more mixed results. Some of these depictions have been subtle and moving; Brian Michael Bendis's quiet restoration of Gwen to Peter in the alternate reality of the "House of M" stands out in this regard.[45] Others are interesting, even as failures; for example, Jeph Loeb and Tim Sale's graphic novel, *Spider-Man: Blue*, is weakened by its sentimentality, but nevertheless bears incidental witness to the attractive pleasure-pain of false nostalgia—surely one of the more dangerous and seductive guises that any trauma can adopt. The relative popularity of this book suggests that fans prefer to remember "good-girl-Gwen" over the more complex Gwen-that-was, for reasons that will bear examination.[46]

The depth of the fans' investment in a falsely idealized vision of Gwen as Peter's perfect-but-lost love is confirmed not only by the success of relatively weak tales like *Spider-Man: Blue*, but by the outrage and hostility provoked by a more ambitious arc: J. Michael Straczynski and Mike Deodato's "Sins Past." This storyline complicated the sentimental memory of Gwen with the revelation that, in a moment of weakness, she was once unfaithful to Peter with Norman Osborn, the man who would later target her for assault in the guise of the Green Goblin.[47] The online reaction of male fans was predictable, if surprising in its intensity: some angrily accused Gwen of being a slut; some attacked Straczynski, as if protecting the reputation of their own spouse or daughter from a vicious scandalmonger; still others tried to rationalize Gwen's behavior within the established continuity of the series, in order to preserve her "goodness" as much as possible.[48] Eventually, even Straczynski himself publicly disowned the story, describing it as compromised by editorial interference.[49] But flawed though it may be, "Sins Past" at least helps to clarify the nature of the fantasy Gwen embodies by making the question of her sexual purity a central issue. Straczynski's Gwen thereby provides some final insight into why her death was so shattering. Straczynski's troubled tale can therefore bring us to a deeper understanding of the symbolic weight attached to the young, female victim.

The problem that needs to be explained is why it is so often the pointless death of a young woman that throws the surviving characters of a story, or the audience of that story, into a traumatic encounter with life's "absurdity." After all, if the desire is to demonstrate the existential condition of mankind through a confrontation with the problem of divine injustice, why should a pretty girl be the preferred sacrificial choice? Why not a morally virtuous man, or a child, or even a baby—the most proverbially innocent of creatures? Why the insistence on the death of a young woman in her reproductive prime, not a just a significant other but also a potential mother? The question is rendered even more pointed in the context of the Spider-Man mythos, because the repetitive structure whereby Peter renounces and then reluctantly returns to the role of hero has often been linked to the fatal loss of a supporting character. Between the deaths of Uncle Ben and Gwen, Spider-Man loses Betty Brant's brother Bennett, the investigative journalist Frederick Foswell, and Gwen's own father, Captain George Stacy. This is a surprisingly high number of fatalities for a superhero title of the Silver Age—and alongside these events we can also consider the aged Aunt May's frequent near-death experiences. Peter feels an inordinate amount of responsibility for all these tragedies, just as he does for Ben's death. And yet not one of these deaths or near-deaths would have the impact of Gwen's death on Peter, his creators, or his fans. Only Gwen's loss seems to have been traumatic enough to force Peter into new understanding of the relationship between power and responsibility. Only Gwen's death functions as a repetition-with-a-difference.

There are, of course, numerous possible answers to this question, since numerous cultural, social, political, and even biological factors may well be in play. But I am attracted to the hints provided by the theoretical encounter between feminism and psychoanalysis, with it's particular emphasis on the conflicted desires of the child during what has come to be known as the pre-oedipal stage.[50] During this hypothetical developmental phase, the child's individuation from the mother is presumed to be incomplete. The child will therefore experience a complex range of sensations and fantasies in relation to the mother's body. For example, being held and nursed may result in the dissolution of the boundaries of self, an experience that may be pleasurable, but can also be anxiety-producing; similarly, separation from the mother may be both sought after and feared. These child-hood experiences and fantasies, it is said, subsequently shape our adult experiences and fantasies with regard to our choices of ideal love-object. In other words, it is during the pre-oedipal phase, and in relation to the mother's body, that we learn our first lessons about the unending tension between dependency and vulnerability, between desire and anxiety, or, more simply still, between love and fear. (More negatively, one might hypothesize further that obsessive or control-ling love relationships in adulthood are in part a belated response to terrors experienced in infancy, terrors that fueled the anxious child's drive to control the mother's body as its source of nurturing bliss.) The point to be grasped is that all love relationships, however "healthy" or well negotiated, are to some extent shaped by the pri-mary anxieties that emerge from the pre-oedipal experience of mater-nal nurture.

Consequently, the destruction of a kind, nurturing, idealized woman violates more than the fantasy that we live in a just universe, where virtuous action receives its due reward. Another, perhaps still more fundamental fantasy is under attack: the fantasy of romance, born out of the anxious longings of the pre-oedipal stage. In the most familiar form of this romantic fantasy, the solution to all of life's problems is not superpower—not strength or flight or agility or invisibility. Instead, the solution is to be found in an endlessly satisfying, sustaining, and healing relationship with a perfect partner, with whom one recreates the pre-oedipal illusion of an ideal union. This psychoanalytic account explains the insatiable demand for "happy endings" that provide the dominant form of closure within countless stories, both comedic and dramatic, from ancient times to the present, from the humblest folktale to the Hollywood blockbuster.

In a culture where the tools of representation are by-and-large in the hands of white heterosexual males, it should be no surprise if the fantasy of a perfect partner is "best" emblematized by an idealized vision of white, youthful femininity: a pretty blonde. But behind this fantasy there is another: the fantasy of pre-oedipal union, which is itself a response to the primal pain of individuation, the ordinary narcissistic wounds of human development. It is therefore important both to recognize the gendered component of our idealized "romance" fantasies, and at the same time to recognize that "they spring from the ground of an infantile experience that is prior to gender."[51] It may be tempting to dismiss the idealization of Gwen Stacy within the comic book community as just another distressing manifestation of a typically heterosexist logic, wherein the overvaluation of an impossibly "good" girl justifies the denigration of women in general. It may be tempting to dismiss the outrage of male fans at Gwen Stacy's infidelity in "Sins Past" along similar lines. But as Janet Adelman has written, in the context of Shakespeare's *King Lear*: ". . . gendered rage at female sexuality in part figures and in part covers over and defends against the more primitive pain of pre-oedipal betrayal, the betrayal inherent in individuation itself . . . [T]he fantasies enacted in Cordelia's loss and return . . . derive from the very beginnings of nascent selfhood, before consciousness and the gender divide."[52]

In my opinion, the very same fantasies are enacted in Gwen's loss, and in the repeated efforts to bring about her return. Like Lear, confronted with Cordelia's corpse, but insisting that she still breathes, many comic book readers and creators simply cannot let Gwen go. Gwen Stacy may be an all-too-typical object of heterosexual male desire, then, but the painful feelings of separation and the longing for blissful merger that she emblematizes are hardly unique to straight men.

This goes some way to explaining why both men and women, of any sexual orientation, might still feel the desire to see Cordelia restored to Lear, or Gwen restored to Peter—even while recognizing (and regretting) the degree to which both characters are asked to give up their individuality and autonomy in order to take up the "good girl" mantle. Further echoing Adelman on *King Lear*, I would suggest that the task of criticism therefore cannot be simply to dismiss the symbolic power of the female victim as a function of the sickness of patriarchy—because while that is no doubt part of the explanation, a more universal expression of painful human yearning also helps to render that symbolism so powerful. Consequently, the critical task must be "simultaneously to acknowledge this place of common need, *and* to measure its cost to the women forced to bear its burden."[53]

The cost to Gwen could be no higher. But the common need she emblematizes, those universal feelings of separation, and the yearning for connection, explain why I myself have been driven to place her at the center of this argument. For I must confess, though it may already by obvious, I too am 'haunted' by Gwen Stacy. I too am vulnerable to the romantic idealism that she represents. I gave up on the fantasy of superpowers long ago, but the fantasy of an endlessly fulfilling, healing, compensatory, perfect love has proved much harder to renounce. And, conversely, the more complex reality—the fact that we are all condemned to love not perfect partners, but ordinary, mortal, and necessarily imperfect human beings—is much harder to embrace. But if in this respect I am like Peter, like his creators, and like his readers, I want at least to claim it is because we are all alike in this. Perhaps, if the psychoanalysts are right, we are alike because in our earliest infancy we dreamed the same dream of perfection, and experienced the same anxiety at separation. Perhaps, if the psychoanalysts are right, true growth requires the destruction of childhood dreams as much as their realization.

But if I am reluctant to let Gwen go, then, it is because I am reluctant to renounce the romantic fantasy of a perfect union, in exchange for more profound challenges, and less certain rewards. If I am reluctant to let Gwen go, it is because I barely know how to love anyone, outside of the terms of the romantic fantasy of a perfect union. To love another despite his or her limitations, dependencies, and imperfections, and indeed, despite our own—is this not one of the hardest things life requires of us? And yet, what other choice is there, when limitation, dependency, and imperfection are our common human inheritance? What other choice is there, when mortality may simply be the most painful human imperfection of all? Certainly, in the context of a profound confrontation with this common inheritance, it should be no cause for wonder if we need stories about heroes that explore the reality of human weakness over and alongside the fantasy of superhuman power. Nor should it be a surprise if somewhere beneath the surface of these stories the dream or the hope of a love that loves despite all weakness and imperfection—a love divine—continues to thrive.

CHAPTER FOUR

IRON MAN: TECHNO-FAITH

1

Let's take a slightly different tack, and begin with the sex scene in the first of the recent *Iron Man* movies. No, not the one between millionaire industrialist Tony Stark (Robert Downey Jr) and *Vanity Fair* reporter Christine Everhart (Leslie Bibb), a brief encounter that starts out as an argument about the ethics of arms dealing and ends with Ms. Everhart receiving a brusque brush off at the hands of Tony's personal assistant, Pepper Potts (Gwyneth Paltrow). That episode is not unimportant, of course; in narrative terms, it efficiently establishes the lifestyle and values of the main protagonist prior to his transformation into Iron Man, marking him as magnificently self-involved, hedonistic, superficial, dismissive of others, and surrounded by willing enablers. But ironically, the sex in *that* scene is significant only to the extent that it is "meaningless"—that is, without commitment, intimacy, or emotional connection, without any exposure of the interior self of either party. For meaning-full sex, we have to wait until Tony returns from Afghanistan, injured by shrapnel, with a miniaturized arc reactor of his own design implanted in his chest to power his damaged heart.

Summoning Pepper to his side, Tony asks her to help him replace this reactor with an upgraded version, in a delicate procedure that requires her to place her hand inside his body through the cybernetic portal in his chest in order to remove a stray piece of wiring. For most of the scene the two actors are positioned side by side in dual close up against a relatively dark background; Tony reclines at an angle, naked from the waist up, while Pepper leans over him. The mood lighting and fixed frame create the atmosphere of a more traditional Hollywood love scene, reinforcing our sense of the privacy and proximity of the couple as they talk easily, in lowered voices. Tony gently cajoles Pepper into going along with the strange request he has made, like a lover trying to persuade a reluctant partner to try something unfamiliar. She gingerly reaches out toward the metal-lined hole in his chest, but then pulls back, uncertain that she is qualified for this task. Tony reassures her that she is not only qualified, but is also the most trustworthy person he has ever met. Trusting to his trust in her, Pepper then inserts her hand into Tony's body, up to the wrist. The action is accompanied by wet, squelching sounds, and by gasps and quickened breathing from both actors. Pepper cries out in disgust that "there's pus!" but Tony again reassures her, insisting that the secretions she has encountered are merely an "inorganic plasmic discharge." "It smells!" Pepper points out, and Tony agrees it does. Attempting to lift the wire, Pepper touches the "socket wall" of Tony's chest cavity, causing him to cry out in shock. She also accidentally pulls out part of the original device, and Tony announces that they must move quickly to insert the replacement unit if he is to avoid going into cardiac arrest.

From its hesitant beginnings, the scene now takes on a new urgency. Pepper stares directly into Tony's eyes and assures him that everything will be OK, before boldly plunging her hand into his chest for a second time to attach the new reactor. Tony shouts again as the mechanical connection is made, this time a kind of yowl that suggests intense pleasure as much as pain. He then relaxes, smiling broadly, relieved and pleased. "That was fun, wasn't it?" he says. Pepper also laughs while insisting that Tony can never "ever, ever, ever," ask her to do something like that again. But Tony refuses to make such a promise. "I don't have anyone but you," he confesses, seductively—and then offers a rueful half-grin, as if acknowledging the sad fact of his own loneliness, before taking up a towel to wipe the sticky residue of the insertion procedure from his belly.

Literal-minded viewers, and those trained by the dominant conventions of modern pornography to partition the sexual from the emotional, will doubtless object that this is not a sex scene at all; but to the less imaginatively limited, the erotic resonances are surely impossible to miss. Of course, it might strike some as a perverse eroticism— "cyborg sex . . . uncoupled from organic reproduction," a disturbing collision of the fleshly and the mechanical that also and perhaps not uncoincidentally happens to reverse the "normal" heterosexual dynamic in which the male penetrates the female.[1]

Certainly, it would not take much imagination to read Pepper's insertion of her hand into Tony's well-lubricated chest cavity as an upwardly displaced figure for the act of anal fisting—something that several theorists of sexuality have argued is particularly taboo for traditional heterosexual males, implying as it does both extreme physical vulnerability and the potentially ego-shattering experience of total abandonment to bodily pleasure. The ancient fantasy of the invulnerable and radically independent warrior-male so brilliantly reconfigured in the modern fantasy of Iron Man's armor—hard, impenetrable, and with the military capability of a tank and a jet combined—would seen to transform here into its necessarily repressed opposite, in the image of a weak, needy, immobile, nakedly exposed man, desperately asking a young woman to penetrate him with her "feminine, petite" hands.

The oppositions of machine and man, autonomy and dependence, and power and vulnerability that are evoked and undone in this emblematic episode will be my main focus in the following pages. I begin by showing how the contradictory impulses of techno-desire and techno-fear have been central themes of the series since it first began, in 1963. I then consider the origins of this complex technological phantasmatic in the intellectual culture of modernity, and particularly in a (loosely) humanist ideology, characterized by what I call "techno-faith"—that is, a fundamental belief in the power of the human will to transform the world to reflect human desires, through the agency of technology; I also reflect on the persistence of this ideology in the contemporary discourse of posthumanism. Returning to Iron Man, I then discuss the ways in which these concepts of autonomy, agency, and the technologically extended will are complicated within several key Iron Man stories in which techno-faith gives way to a more reflective techno-skepticism. These stories also enlarge our perspective on technological dependence by examining the issue through the lens of Tony Stark's alcohol dependence. Then, in a final section, I consider the "spiritual" philosophy of Alcoholic's Anonymous—a fellowship that nowadays counts Tony Stark as a member—as a "post-secular" response to the excesses of liberal humanism.

2

In the early 1960s, the Cold War was heating up on several fronts— quite literally, in Vietnam, but also in imaginative terms around the concept of technology. As both ubiquitous features of the modern landscape and vivid symbols of future possibility, the innovations of postwar technology were always more than versatile solutions for contemporary living. The automobiles, televisions, transistor radios, refrigerators, washing machines, and other household gadgets that became available for mass consumption in the United States of the 1950s were also widely heralded as evidence for the social and political superiority of that nation.

This fusion of political ideology with the promise of technology was most vividly apparent in the space race. The competition between the United States and the USSR to be first to reach the moon was no doubt in part driven by the noble impulse of scientific discovery. But those rockets, spacesuits, and lunar buggies were also extremely expensive technological props in a spectacular piece of political theater. (To acknowledge the enormous propaganda coup of the moon landing is to recognize the kernel of truth at the heart of the conspiracy theory, still advanced by some, that it was quite literally staged.) Against this background, the idea of technology inevitably took on what the psychoanalysts call a phantasmatic function within American consciousness—which is to say, that it was not only an increasingly central concept around which fantasies of national identity coalesced but also a particularly fertile site for the projection of desire and her nervous twin, anxiety.

Perhaps unsurprisingly, then, Marvel's most technologically enhanced Silver Age superhero was also the most politically hawkish. Iron Man made his debut in March of 1963, and from very first pages of his origin story—set in the jungles of Vietnam—his adventures were stridently anticommunist. Indeed, from our present historical distance, the glorious political simplicity of these early tales could almost be part of their charm, were it not for the frequent racial stereotyping of Iron Man's enemies from the various "red" nations (a failure of the creative imagination that is all the more marked in contrast to other aspects of the series). But although the early *Iron Man* comic books are most kindly described as naïve in political terms, the attitudes and fantasies they express with regard to technology are often more sophisticated and ambivalent; and on occasion, this ambivalence toward technology complicates the ostensibly straightforward political agenda of the stories.

Take for example, *Tales of Suspense* #46 (October, 1962), which opens with a caricature of Nikita Khrushchev—brilliantly portrayed by Don Heck, one of Marvel's most underrated Silver Age artists—in dialog with a Russian version of Tony Stark named Ivan Vanko, who has invented his own armored costume and taken up the identity of The Crimson Dynamo. Khrushchev's thought balloons make it clear that he regards Vanko as a threat to his own power, tolerating him only reluctantly, for the sake of his scientific expertise. After witnessing a demonstration of Vanko's powers as the Dynamo, Khrushchev sends him on a mission to ruin Tony Stark, imagining that he will either destroy or be destroyed by Iron Man—a win-win situation from the Soviet Leader's Machiavellian perspective. Vanko almost succeeds in ruining Stark by secretly wrecking several of his manufacturing plants. As a consequence of this destruction, the US military loses faith in Stark's capacity to deliver the sophisticated weapons they need from him. Potentially deprived of his lucrative defense contracts, Stark worries that he will be broken financially. To make matters worse, in a remarkable depiction of Cold War paranoia, certain members of the US government then begin to worry that Tony Stark may himself be a communist agent, sabotaging his own factories! A group of bowtie wearing members of the Senate speculate in horrified tones about the possibility. "If Stark is a communist agent, look at the sweet spot he's in!" declares one. "First he grabs up dozens of government contracts! This makes the U.S. heavily dependent on his industrial empire for strategic weapons and research! Then he wrecks his own plants! Result? . . . We fall behind the Communists. . . ."

"By George! If you're right . . ." worries another, before adding ominously "we have to investigate Stark thoroughly!!" (See Figure 4.1.)

Of course, Stark eventually clears his name and defeats the Dynamo by using a (faked) recording to trick him into believing that Khrushchev intends to "liquidate" him upon his return to Russia. This is not quite an outright lie, for Khrushchev is depicted as thinking along these lines, although Iron Man has no way of knowing this beyond his conviction that all communists are "treacherous." Vanko reacts by embracing Iron Man as an ally and defecting to the United States—much to the fury of Khrushchev, who appears in the final panel of the story, hurling objects around his Kremlin office in an outburst of infantile rage.[2]

At one level, the story is obviously a propagandist attempt to allay American fears over the threat of Russian military technology by

Figure 4.1 A depiction of Cold War paranoia from *Tales of Suspense* #46. © Marvel Comics.

showing that the values of pluck, ingenuity, and (relative) trustworthiness will overcome even the most sophisticated enemy innovations. It also allows the patriotic reader to have his technological cake and eat it too, as it were, suggesting by means of Vanko's defection that the most brilliant foreigners will ultimately recognize the superiority of the American way and assimilate—so "their" technology ends up becoming "ours," anyway. But by depending as it does on the assumption that "all commies are chronically suspicious of each other," Iron Man's victory is finally depicted as a consequence of the moral superiority of the USA, rather than technological superiority (the status of which is less certain). This conclusion underscores the ambiguous attitude toward technology manifested throughout the comic.

Although it is the source of Iron Man's power, technology does not function here as a simple ideological panacea, but is rather presented as a source of anxiety for politicians within both the capitalist *and* the communist systems. The fear and resentment of *both* forms of political leadership with regard to the prospect of technological dependency turn out to be the real sources of drama and danger—lying behind both Khrushchev's manipulations of the Crimson Dynamo and the more familiar homegrown terrors of senatorial inquisition and financial bankruptcy that threaten to overwhelm Tony during the paranoid peak of this Cold War adventure. The simpleminded patriotism of the story is thus complicated in an intriguing way by its more nuanced, ambivalent exploration of the technological phantasmatic.

This ambivalence towards technology—desired as a source of power, but feared and resented, as the cause of a crippling dependency for those who rely upon it—is not confined to this one early tale. It is actually a fundamental element of the original version of the Iron Man character—built into his armor, we might say, in the form of his chest plate, which is not only the main energy source for the suit, but also prevents the inoperable fragments of shrapnel embedded in his chest during his days in Vietnam from reaching his heart and killing him. Tony Stark's very life depends on this piece of equipment; consequently, he can never remove it, making it a resonant symbol of the double-edged nature of his techno-dependence, as well as a literal barrier to intimacy (and hence something of an impediment to his former playboy lifestyle). During Stan Lee's tenure as writer for the character, this chest plate frequently functioned—or rather malfunctioned—as a plot device. Over-taxing himself during superheroic combat, Iron Man would be left in urgent need of a "recharge" for his chest plate; he consequently spent an inordinate amount of time staggering around in agonizing pain while searching desperately for a power source. Both a blessing and a curse, the engine of his strength and the point of his greatest weakness, Iron Man's chest plate is therefore readily legible as an unconscious emblem for the mixed feelings of the nation with regard to the effects of scientific and technological progress.

But for all its symbolic resonance, the threat of "chest plate failure" could only be used as a plot device so many times before it lost its capacity to generate suspense. So it was that when Archie Goodwin succeeded Stan Lee as writer of the Iron Man comic in the late 1960s, he contrived to have Tony undergo a new form of experimental heart surgery, finally removing the Vietnam shrapnel, and ostensibly freeing him from his most spectacular symptom of techno-dependence. Nevertheless, the dangers of technological dependence remained a fundamental theme of the series. For example, from the beginning of his run, most of Goodwin's villains were as likely to fall victim to their own destructive technology as they were to be defeated by Iron Man.[3] But Goodwin also explored more socially relevant variations on the theme of technology gone awry. Among the most memorable of these was *Iron Man* #25 (May, 1970), which contained a prescient tale about the environmental destruction that can follow upon the relentless pursuit of cheap energy. Entitled "This Doomed Land, This Dying Sea," and magnificently illustrated by former EC artist, Johnny Craig, the story is framed by a presentation made by Tony Stark to his peers in the industrial-corporate world. In this framing sequence, Stark argues that the sun's rays are interacting with pollutants in the atmosphere to effect global air quality, a problem that will worsen as our ever more contaminated oceans start to die.[4] Predictably, his concerns fall on deaf ears. "We're businessmen, not philanthropists," declares one member of the audience, while another dismisses Stark's claim as "just a theory." "Who knows what will really happen in ten or thirty years?" says yet another. Perhaps even more disturbingly familiar is the sequence wherein the Sub-Mariner discovers a huge pipe leaking black and purple plumes of toxic chemicals into the depths of the ocean—images that now inevitably evoke the horrific consequences of the explosion at BP's Deepwater Horizon oil well in the Gulf of Mexico in April of 2010. The overall message of Goodwin's story, unblunted by the local success of Iron Man and the Sub-Mariner in containing this particular environmental hazard, is that the combined impact of our technological and economic dependence on the world's natural resources threatens the survival of the planet, and that corporate cost-cutting measures are increasing the likelihood of an unprecedented disaster.[5]

In the mid 1970s, writer Bill Mantlo extended Goodwin's reflections on the relationship between unthinking capitalist ideology and technological destructiveness into the realm of foreign policy. As more Americans began to question the validity and purpose of the Vietnam War, so did Iron Man; and Tony Stark's history as a designer of weapons used in that specific theater of combat became a focus of painful introspection on the part of the character in Mantlo's "Long Time Gone," from *Iron Man* #78 (September, 1975). "What kind of man was I to keep designing weaponry for that kind of war?" Stark asks himself, before flashing back to his last visit to Vietnam as a combatant—a trip taken as Iron Man to oversee the function of a hyperaccurate rocket launcher of his own design. The story itself takes aim at the notion that advances in military technology can speed up the pace of a conflict, thereby saving lives in the longer run. Stark's new weapon may hold out "the promise of a faster kill, a well-oiled war," but it is immediately deployed in a secret mission, "violating international law," and as such is morally compromised from the start. In the course of this mission, the super-gun works horribly effectively, killing large numbers of enemy troops; but when it is destroyed by an aircraft attack, its crew have nothing more to protect them than conventional small arms, and, out-numbered, they too are massacred. ("They didn't have a chance once my gun was knocked out," Stark tells us.) Thus, while the technology functions precisely as intended, it also fosters a flagrant disregard for the rule of law and a self-destructive dependence in those who possess it, while encouraging vicious retaliation on the part of those who don't. In other words, all Stark's invention finally does is increase the number of victims on both sides. Shocked into awareness by this experience—one that he barely survives—Iron Man constructs a mass grave for the enemy soldiers that his gun has killed, emblazoned with the word "WHY?" Returning to Stark in the present, we see him reflect on the lives that "have been lost through the ignorance of men like the man I once was." The story also makes clear that Stark has now distanced himself from the work of the military industrial complex, closing down the weapons division of his company. Nowadays his "business is peace, pure and simple, and a betterment of man through technology."[6]

To summarize thus far, then: while it might be tempting to dismiss Iron Man's early adventures as simplistic, conservative Cold War propaganda, grounded in a comforting fantasy about superior American scientific ingenuity, such an analysis would be reductive. In fact, from his very earliest adventures, the Iron Man character is a walking metaphor for the contradictory impulses of techno-desire and techno-fear that form part of the psychological furniture in the mental house of modern liberalism. Moreover, as the series progressed, different creators would explore this contradiction with increasing levels of sophistication and awareness.

3

Up to now, I have proceeded as if the phantasmatic function of technology were a distinctively American, postwar phenomenon. But our contemporary technological fantasies have deep historical roots, stretching back at least as far as the eighteenth century, with broader implications for our understanding of Western intellectual culture.

If we take a step back for a moment to think about these roots and implications, we will see that there is still more at stake in the Iron Man fantasy than we may have at first recognized.

Philosopher Kate Soper has criticized the intellectual ideology of late modernity for its tendency to embrace the logic of what she calls " 'technical fix' humanism," something she sees as a grotesque reduction or corruption of the principles of Enlightenment rationalism. According to Soper, this ideology "approaches human affairs on the model of the industrial enterprise [with its] . . . continual subordination of natural resources and human talents to values of growth and economic prosperity." The unexamined bedrock assumption here is that human "happiness is . . . achieved not through the alteration of values or of the 'needs' they breed and endorse, but by organizing the environment in such a way that it corresponds more closely to . . . [our] demands."

As Soper acknowledges, this " 'technical fix' humanism has little in common" with the most sophisticated philosophizing of the Enlightenment, let alone with the literary humanism of the Italian Renaissance. But she nevertheless insists that "a profound confidence in our powers to come to know and thereby control our environment and destiny lies at the heart of every humanism," and "in this sense we must acknowledge a continuity of theme" in this strain of Western thought, "however warped it may have become with the passage of time." She goes on to add:

> We can trace a similar continuity of theme in the anti-theological component of humanist thought. For while Renaissance humanism by no means implied any overt attack on religion of the kind we associate with the period of the Enlightenment, the anticlericalism of the latter has its roots in the resistance to medieval church dogma that was characteristic of the Italian movement; and the hardening of this resistance into a committed atheism goes along with a progressive confirmation of humanity's powers of self-determination in the development of science and its successful application . . . Francis Bacon's assumption that it is only "vain notions and blind experiments" that forbid "a happy match between the mind of man and the nature of things," was to find repeated justification in the astonishing capacity of homo sapiens to harness nature in the service of its own ends—a capacity that

appeared increasingly to distance it from any other species inhab-
iting the planet—and to bear daily witness to the truth that
"man" is indeed "the measure of all things."[7]

In short, " 'technical-fix' humanism" not only battens on the wither-
ing of traditional religious belief structures, but emerges from a historical paradigm shift in the western understanding of the world
and our place within it—very broadly speaking, a movement from
the medieval system of faith in "Providence" to the rationalist logic
of "progress" (to use Hegel's influential terms from his *Lectures on
the Philosophy of World History*). The technological fantasy that
undergirds Iron Man's adventures is therefore more than a product
of the postwar politics and society of the United States; it is a promi-
nent feature of the psychological landscape of modernity itself.

However, as another contemporary philosopher, Susan Neiman,
has pointed out, despite the massive intellectual transformation
implied by this historical shift, the paradigms of Providence and
progress are structurally similar insofar as they are both responses
to the same perennial difficulty. Theologians named this difficulty
"the problem of evil" centuries ago, but for contemporary readers
unfamiliar with the conventions of theological discourse it might be
less confusingly called "the problem of human suffering."[8]

Under the paradigm of Providence, human suffering is assumed
to have a purpose—as a punishment for sin, for example, or as an
inducement to moral development and growth. Apparently meaningless suffering is therefore *only* apparent. Although some events
may appear beyond human comprehension, they are all part of God's
mysterious plan. One day we too will understand, but that knowledge will be revealed to us in the next world, not this one. Under the
paradigm of progress, on the other hand, human suffering is explained
as a consequence of ignorance. We can therefore mitigate it through
the application of the tools of reason, and one day, when we have
achieved a sufficiently penetrating knowledge of the physical laws
and abstract principles that govern the disposition of matter and
morality, we can hope to alleviate suffering altogether. But as Neimen
argues, despite the different assumptions that structure these different paradigms, both finally "posit an order counter to the mess that
experience presents."[9] That is, they both presume the existence of a
world that makes sense, somewhere behind or beyond the random,

chaotic world of appearances—and both hold out a deferred promise of access to that meaningful, ordered world.

Thus, the hermeneutic systems of Providence and progress can *both* be characterized as faith-based at a basic level, but with different ideas about the source of divinity. Within the first system the object of worship is the Judeo-Christian God, and within the second, the object of worship is Man, or more precisely, Man's reason—and by extension, the scientific and technological fruits of that reason. As Hegel would put it: "Armed with the concept of reason, we need not fear coming to grips with any subject whatsoever."[10] As Neiman shows, the great philosophers of modernity, a list that includes Hegel, as well as Kant and Marx, were well aware of "the continuities between sacred and secular concepts even as they undertook to transform them."[11] Today, by contrast, many self-professed secular humanists fail to recognize the deep structural similarity between the belief in Providence that they (often scornfully) reject and the belief in scientific progress to which they are (often uncritically) devoted. They fail to see that their " 'technical fix' humanism" does not so much leave religion behind as replicate one primary aspect of its traditional function: to mitigate the experience of human suffering by "making sense" of existence. But in the light of Neiman's analysis, " 'technical fix' humanism" is no less a form of faith than a more traditional, God-centered religion. It is, precisely, techno-faith.

Of course, modernity has also produced its share of discontents. As Brent Waters has written:

> The axis of industry, science, and technology . . . admittedly generated unprecedented prosperity. The distribution of wealth, however, was far from even. The cost of industrialization was the emergence of widespread poverty, deplorable working conditions, squalid cities, political corruption, and devastated rural communities and landscapes. Mastering nature was a violent conquest, encompassing the collateral damage of appalling numbers of decimated families and communities. Exchanging the pain and misery of an inscrutable providence for that of willful exploitation was proving, for many, to be a bad bargain. The science which had promised to liberate humans from the shackles of superstition and fossilized tradition was instead serving as a cruel, industrial taskmaster. For many, there was little difference between the

medieval serfs tied to the estates of their lords, and modern laborers chained to the factories of their employers.[12]

As the excesses of industrialization gave way to the greater horrors of postindustrial warfare in the early-twentieth century, even the most optimistic technologists must have sometimes begun to wonder if their faith was misplaced. Moreover, new discoveries within the fields of psychology and biology complicated and even undermined the notion of Reason itself. As Waters writes, ". . . the Darwinian and Freudian glimpses into the human psyche suggested that . . . [h]uman behavior did not evolve along any discernible providential or progressive trajectories, but adapted to changing environments."[13] Consequently, by the mid-twentieth century, it increasingly appeared to many that the human story was neither a matter of Providence nor progress but was rather an essentially random *process*. It is in the context of this third paradigm shift in our self-understanding that we can begin to understand the claims for "anti-humanism" that have become common among postwar intellectuals.

At the risk of over-simplification, we might summarize the foregoing account by saying that while the intellectual conditions of modernity were shaped by a crisis of faith in God, the intellectual conditions of postmodernity have been shaped by a crisis of faith in Man.[14] And if one name for that faith in Man is humanism, then it should come as no surprise to learn that many contemporary thinkers nowadays style themselves as *antihumanists*—and that some even call themselves *posthumanists*. Of course, just as "humanism" is an umbrella term, imprecisely covering a number of different and sometimes contradictory intellectual responses to the widespread decline of the belief in Providence, so the various discourses labeled *antihumanist* and *posthumanist* actually describe a number of different and contradictory responses to the logic of progress. To describe the full range of antihumanist philosophies would require a separate book, or even a multivolume series; but following the work of N. Katherine Hayles, we can perhaps identify a few characteristic posthuman assumptions, at least insofar as they have been articulated within the arenas of popular science writing and contemporary speculative science fiction (two different but always closely related genres).

In general, scientific posthumanists understand the universe in primarily informational terms; or as Hayles puts it, they privilege "informational pattern over material instantiation." This particular conception of the priority of information can be clarified by means of an analogy. Consider the various technologies for the recording and playback of music that have appeared in the last 100 years or so. Apparently, the same recording can be preserved in the groves of a wax cylinder or vinyl disc, or as oxidized particles on tape, or as digital code on a compact disc or computer. The musical "information" that makes up the song can therefore be regarded as the primary content, while the different forms of cylinder, disc, tape, or electronic file are merely more or less interchangeable means of containing and transmitting that information. The challenge comes in moving the song from one material substrate to the next, without losing any of the information that constitutes it, and without replicating noises that were a function of the inherent limitations of its particular materialization—the surface noise of a wax platter, the hiss of tape moving over recording heads, and so on.

It is this conception of information as the primary and ultimately immaterial content of the universe that underwrites a characteristically dismissive posthuman attitude toward the body as little more than the "original prosthesis" for the mind.[15] To put it in terms of the music analogy, the mind is the song, and the flesh just a wax cylinder. Once relegated to the secondary status of a mere storage container, the body is readily subject to the modernist-capitalist logic of obsolescence, so that it becomes possible to think in terms of enhancing it or even replacing it with a superior technological innovation—upgrading it just as one might upgrade the "software" of one's record collection, from fragile and heavy vinyl to more permanent and portable digital files.[16] Obviously, such notions have been the stuff of science fiction for decades—critics usually cite the work of William Gibson here, but one might also point to earlier stories by Philip K. Dick and James Tiptree, Jr. But more recently, certain members of the scientific community, particularly those involved in computer science and robotics, have debated these kinds of ideas (and related posthuman fantasies, such as the coming of "the Singularity") with surprising seriousness. For the most grandiose of these posthuman scientists, such as Ray Kurzweil, the process of technological self-transformation is nothing short of an evolutionary necessity—and if it also represents the end of humanity as we know it, then this is a consummation devoutly to be wished:

Evolution moves toward greater complexity, greater elegance, greater knowledge, greater intelligence, greater beauty, greater creativity, greater love. And God has been called all these things. . . . Evolution does not achieve an infinite level, but as it explodes exponentially it certainly moves in this direction. . . . Thus, the freeing of our thinking from the severe limitations of its biological form may be regarded as an essentially spiritual quest.[17]

Many commentators have noted Kurzweil's theological vocabulary with some irony, as if the mere invocation of God in the context of a "futurist" project were inherently contradictory; however, this is not a very telling criticism, since the position he articulates is hardly traditionally religious, but more loosely mystical. He does not say that human beings should strive to *know* God, after all, but rather that by imbuing inorganic machines with human consciousness, we can *become* Godlike ourselves: immortal, all-knowing, and near omnipotent in our creative manipulations of the universal data-stream. But theorists working within the humanities rather than Kurzweil's fields of technology and robotics have also been quick to point out that while this account of the future may be posthuman, it is not exactly post*humanist*. After all, isn't this vision of mankind ascendant on artificial wings the very dream of humanism, articulated in more explicitly techno-theological terms than ever before? And moreover, if the unexamined assumptions of humanism brought us to our current pass, then how high might the cost be of this posthuman adventure—or rather, this disavowed humanist technological fantasy?

A significant counter-strand of posthumanist discourse has therefore been devoted to unmasking the residual humanism that lurks behind the posthuman dream of Kurzweil and his ilk.[18] In fact, by now, the spectacle of posthumanist theorists accusing one another of being little more than humanists in cyborg costumes has become familiar to the point of tedium. But such arguments have had the helpful effect of making clear that certain humanist assumptions regarding the nature of the self, and the autonomy of the human will, are much harder to escape—or do without—than we imagine. For example, to the extent that any happy vision of the posthuman future assumes that "we" will always have a measure of conscious, autonomous, control over the tools of technology, that vision would seem to presume the persistence of the liberal humanist subject in some form or other, however disembodied. Even Hayles, whose own work is largely devoted to unmasking the residual humanism of posthumanists like Kurzweil, Hans Moravec, and others, has been criticized for presuming the existence (or persistence) of an essentially humanist notion of the individual at crucial moments in her own arguments.[19] In fact, the problem is implicit in the very title of her most influential book on the subject, *How We Became Posthuman*. Strictly speaking, if "we" became posthuman, "we" could no longer be what "we" were. But for the project of becoming posthuman to work imaginatively as anything other than a dystopian nightmare, "we" must think of ourselves as somehow remaining ourselves even as we undergo a radical change into something else. Thus, it may be that projecting a posthuman future without importing humanist assumptions about the nature of identity is not merely difficult but actually an impossible challenge.

4

Returning to Iron Man: as may already be obvious to some readers, I think this series can be productively interpreted as an almost 50-year-long pop cultural exploration of the complex moral and intellectual issues that arise out of the movement from late-modernity to post-modernity, from progress to process, and from humanism to posthumanism. From the moment that Tony Stark attached himself to the power supply of his chest plate, it became an open question whether he was an autonomous human being using a machine, or a dependent human being whose autonomy was radically undermined by that same machine, or an entirely new form of creature—a hybrid of man and machine, no longer really "human" at all. Consequently, Iron Man's subsequent adventures have at various times embodied the tensions between technical fix humanism, techno-skepticism, and a more obscurely descried posthuman vision. Frequently, the stories resolve into classically, comfortingly humanist fantasies that reify an idealized conception of "Man." (An almost-too-pat example occurs at the end of *The Invincible Iron Man* #2, when the villainous inventor of a robot designed to destroy the hero realizes the error of his ways. "In all the madness of trying to produce a machine to be the equal of Iron Man, I never saw the real truth," he says, "that no skill could duplicate his most essential powers . . . a human heart and . . . courage!")[20] But the ambivalence surrounding Tony Stark's technological dependence also opened the door to rather more complex accounts of the human—accounts that raised more difficult questions about the nature of human agency as manifested through technology—and it is to a more detailed examination of some of these stories that I shall now turn.

In 1979, the creative team of David Michelinie, Bob Layton, and John Romita Jr, produced one of the two most important and influential story arcs of the entire *Iron Man* series since the origin story, an arc that has since become known as *Demon in a Bottle*, after the title of its culminating chapter. The story begins with the introduction of a subplot in which Stark discovers that severing his ties with the US military is more easily desired than done. The potential value of his research and inventions to the defense industry is simply too great to be overlooked, and so the government makes a clandestine attempt to buy a controlling stock interest in his company. When Stark finds out, he confronts his longtime ally, Nick Fury—head of Shield, the most important government defense organization in the Marvel Universe—only to be told flatly: "America needs Stark International to make munitions." If Tony won't cooperate in that project, the government will have to buy him out, and his longstanding friendship with Nick Fury will not protect him. The dangerous interdependence of technological "innovation" and capitalist economics analyzed in earlier stories by Goodwin and Mantlo here turns out to create forces that are greater than any one individual, and that override traditional alliances based on mutual recognition and respect.

Naturally, Stark is deeply wounded by Fury's betrayal, and his unhappiness is compounded by a series of unexplained technological faults in his Iron Man armor (faults that it will later transpire are the result of interference by a rival corporation, headed by one Justin Hammer, who wants to wipe out Stark International altogether). One of these equipment failures leads to the accidental death of an innocent bystander, and though Iron Man is ultimately cleared of any legal responsibility, Stark must live with the guilt. As his problems mount, he increasingly takes refuge in alcohol, and the occasional boozy floozy. During these brandy-fuelled binges, the angry, narcissistic, and self-pitying aspects of his personality come to the surface. Alienating his closest friends through his behavior, he eventually finds himself alone in his penthouse with just a bottle of liquor and the Iron Man armor for company. Talking to his own helmet, like a drunken Hamlet addressing Yorick's skull, he resolves to give up being Tony Stark and stick with the more enjoyable Iron Man role, before taking off dramatically for a jet-powered flight—and realizing, all too late, that in his befuddled state he neglected to open the window before flying through it.[21]

While this episode is obviously a superheroic allegorization of the alcoholic desire to leave behind the problems and responsibilities of a sometimes less-than-satisfactory life—and also, perhaps, for the dangers of drunken "driving"—the Iron Man armor is also shown to have its own addictive pull for Tony Stark, here. It is a mechanical prop for his wounded ego, and a way for him to avoid himself. More accurately, it is his preferred self—a narcissistic ideal, technologically enhanced, impervious to harm, and brightly colored in crimson and gold. Both Michelinie and Layton have since stated that they initially hit upon alcoholism as a plot element simply as a substitute for the tired dramatic device of the failing chest plate, and that its aptness as a "weakness" was suggested by Stark's career as a high-flying corporate jetsetter. But whether they consciously intended to or not, these writers also hit upon a way of extending the theme of techno-logical dependency into more explicitly psychological territory. As such, Stark's descent into alcoholism enlarged the creators' and readers' perspectives with regard to the underlying techno-fantasy of the series, allowing them to think about his pursuit of technological self-enhancement as itself a form of addiction (see Figure 4.2).

The striking conjunctions between the problem of alcoholism and the negative aspects of the technological fantasy are further empha-sized by the language of substance abuse counseling—a language that indicates that the relationship between techno-dependence and substance addiction is embedded in our most basic descriptive meta-phors. Consider, for example, the notion that alcoholic drinking is distinguished from "normal" drinking when it is used as a coping *mechanism* for dealing with unpleasant emotional states and sensa-tions. Here, the technological metaphor has been so literalized as part of the familiar vocabulary of alcoholism that we might not even notice it at first (hence my use of italics). But for addiction counselors, it can be valuable to reawaken that "dead" mechanical metaphor, as a way of providing the alcoholic with a better understanding of his/her problem. Thus, Roget Lockard describes the alcoholic's relation-ship to alcohol precisely as "the discovery of *a technology of feelings management.*" (Interestingly, Lockard also completes the metaphori-cal loop in the other direction: "It is . . . self-evident," he says, "that the use of military technology provides the use with feeling-states comparable to those available through drinking.")[22]

Figure 4.2 Technological dependency and alcohol dependency figure each other in this sequence from *The Invincible Iron Man* #128. © Marvel Comics.

Tony Stark could not remain disabled by alcoholism and also continue in his career as a superhero; but in newsstand comics of the late 1970s, a realistic depiction of his recovery was probably beyond the capacity of the form.[23] Thus, for most contemporary readers, Tony seems to get well rather rapidly, in just the last few pages of the story in which the window-smashing incident occurs (though not before he makes a few more dangerous errors while piloting his Iron Man armor under-the-influence). But even in this artificially compressed narrative space, certain aspects of the 12-step approach to addiction are touched upon. For example, after having identified the root cause of his drinking in his refusal to share the burden of his emotional pain, Tony first admits his helplessness, and then opens his heart to his trusted friend, Beth Cabe; although not couched in quite the same language, these actions mirror the suggestions of the first and fifth steps of Alcoholics Anonymous, respectively. Later, he is also shown making an "amends" to one of the people he has harmed during his binges, his friend and employee, Jarvis, in what might be a reference to the ninth step.[24]

With the *Demon in a Bottle* storyline, then, Michelinie, Layton, and Romita Jr, reconfigured the issue of technological dependence *and* pointed toward a potential solution to the problem, by exploring the theme of chemical dependence, and drawing out some intriguing parallels between the two. The cure for both forms of dependency, it turns out, is to acknowledge that the fantasies of radical independence—absolute power, total control, complete self-reliance—are just that: fantasies. The answer to the problem of negative dependence is therefore not the pursuit of independence—something that only aggravates the problem—but the radical acceptance of *inter*dependence. Tony Stark must accept that his sense of self cannot be sustained in isolation; at the most literal level, his well-being depends upon his recognition that subjectivity is intersubjective—that the self is only sustained through the act of sharing with others.

In the years that followed the appearance of this widely acclaimed story, the popular psychological understanding of alcohol and drug addiction would play an increasingly significant role in Tony Stark's characterization, and the essentially spiritual injunction to "let go" of the impulse for control underlying most addiction treatments would also be more explicitly addressed. For example, when Michelinie and Layton returned to the *Iron Man* book in the late 1980s, this time collaborating with penciller Mark Bright, they produced another extended storyline known as *Armor Wars*, in which Stark discovers that Justin Hammer has passed on details of the Iron Man technology to dozens of others, including several supervillains, but also certain government agencies such as Shield. Stark is horrified that his designs might have been used for nefarious purposes, but at a deeper level, he seems even more furious that his creations might be used by anyone other than himself. He therefore sets out to recover or destroy every armored suit in the Marvel universe that makes use of Stark technology—regardless of the purposes for which that technology is used. When tackling a villain like the Controller, this is a fairly unproblematic plan; but when this means destroying the equipment of the Guardsmen, a group of security personnel employed by the government at a complex designed to incarcerate supervillains, Stark's logic seems warped. "The Guardsmen themselves aren't evil, but I can't take the chance that their armor could fall into evil hands," he declares—as if this hasn't already happened, and on *his* watch. His assumption that the only safe "hands" are his own is therefore already demonstrably false, as well as arrogant. Moreover, in the pursuit of this dubious attempt to stuff the technological genie back into a bottle (as it were), Stark comes into conflict with old allies such as Nick Fury and even Captain America; and in his dealings with these former friends he is self-centered, obsessive, emotionally manipulative, and flat-out dishonest. He occasionally expresses pangs of conscience about this behavior, but this doesn't stop him from doing what he wants in order to regain the control over the Iron Man technology.[25]

During this period, Stark does not actually drink, although we see him struggling with the desire. His friend and employee James "Rhodey" Rhodes discovers him sitting pensively at the private bar in the headquarters of Stark Enterprises (as his company was then known) staring at his reflection in a bottle. Stark admits to Rhodes that he has "never wanted a drink more," but he also recognizes that it won't actually help his situation, and manages to abstain.[26] However, the popular discourse around addiction tells us that "there is a distinct difference between mere abstinence and sobriety. *Abstinence*, with no change in the control-oriented epistemology, manifests in a very rigid, frequently moralistic and judgmental presentation, and is based on *self-deprivation*. Such a person is often described as a 'dry drunk.'"[27] Whether or not one believes in this notion of the "dry drunk" (and the implications of this belief are considerable, not least because it would seem to make alcoholism into an epistemological error rather than a mental or physical problem), Stark's behavior in *Armor Wars* is obviously consistent with this account, and suggests that in the language of AA, at least, while he may not be drinking, he is far from "sober." Instead, in a psychological paradox that is as surely as mysterious to those who have never experienced it as it must be distressing for those have, Stark has lost control of his impulse to control.

Without needing to evoke the abstractions of postwar antihumanist philosophy regarding the illusory nature of the autonomous liberal subject, then, the introduction of these parallel themes of technological dependence and substance addiction made the reflexive paradox of self-control—the question of who, exactly, can be said to control the self, if not the self— central to the series. The paradox manifested most clearly in *Armor Wars* in the way that the man inside the mechanical suit increasingly seemed to become more obsessive— indeed, more *robotic*—in his responses to the world, even as that suit became more adaptable, expressive, and versatile. Serially dating an endless parade of interchangeable glamorous women, serially redesigning his armor, compulsively struggling to dictate the shape of the world around him when he was not compulsively drinking to escape from it—at such moments, it was Tony Stark whose behavior seemed unthinking, automatic, repetitious, and programmed, while Iron Man seemed caring, happy, and free-spirited by comparison. But if in his uncontrolled efforts at control the very status of Stark's human agency seemed questionable, he seemed to rediscover himself through the agency of technology, experiencing a broader range of human feelings and freedoms from within his artificially engineered alter ego. To this extent, he was perhaps already less superhuman than posthuman.

5

The tension between humanist and posthuman versions of the technological fantasy became a still more explicit theme of the series in the hands of Warren Ellis. Hired by Marvel to reboot the Iron Man character in 2005, Ellis turned in a six-part story called *Extremis*, which was then illustrated in a hyperrealist style by the hugely talented Adi Granov. Aspects of Ellis and Granov's work served as source material for the first *Iron Man* movie, and as such *Extremis* may be the single most influential *Iron Man* story of recent years; but Stark's characterization in the comic is quite different from that of Robert Downey Jr's in the film, and Ellis's explorations of techno-faith and its moral implications are more complex.[28]

Besides moving the Iron Man origin forward from 1960s Vietnam to early twenty-first-century Afghanistan, Ellis reconfigured the personality of Tony Stark for the contemporary era, portraying him as a brilliant futurist who has lost his religion—an inventor caught in a crisis of techno-faith. The origins of this crisis are laid out in the first chapter, when Stark sits for an interview with one John Pillinger (a less-than-thinly veiled surrogate for the distinguished documentary filmmaker and activist, John Pilger). Pillinger presses Stark on his history as an arms dealer, confronting him with evidence that his patented miniaturized "smart bomb" technology failed to operate as designed when deployed during the first Gulf War. Now scattered across the former theaters of conflict, these tiny bombs continue to cause horrific injuries to the civilians unlucky enough to stumble across them. Pillinger also suggests that the Iron Man suit—Stark's most famous invention, of course—is "just a defense industry application."

Stark does not dispute Pillinger's claims regarding his earlier designs, but denies that Iron Man is a weapon, and points out that his initial military funding has since given rise to numerous "social technologies" such as "medical biometric implants, cardiac replacement medicine, and internal analgesic pumps."[29] "I've never claimed to be perfect," he confesses, "I always knew there would be blood on my hands." But nevertheless, he insists, "I'm trying to improve the world."

"Improve the world," Pillinger echoes, the repetition serving to drive home the arrogance and vanity of Stark's position, and the blindness of his former techno-faith. But Pillinger does not quite get the last word. Wrapping things up, he asks Stark, "If you know my work, why did you agree to this interview?"

Stark replies: "I wanted to ask: Have you changed anything? You've been uncovering disturbing things all over the world for 20 years now . . . you've worked very hard . . . intellectuals, critics, and activists follow your work very closely. But culturally, you're almost invisible, Mr. Pillinger. Have you changed anything?"

Granov portrays Pillinger listening to this reply for two separate panels, without responding; the frown on his face indicates that he understands the thrust of Stark's challenge—which is obviously something like "Haven't you have used *your* tools to improve the world? Isn't that *your* goal, too? And what have *you* achieved?" When Pillinger finally responds, the expression Granov gives him is hard to read. He does not seem angry—a slight smile plays over his lips—but his brow is furrowed, his eyes sad. It's a tired, almost rueful expression that allows the reader to hear the hesitation before he finally answers.

"I don't know."

"Me neither," says Stark.

At issue from the beginning of Ellis's take, then, are ethical questions regarding the nature of right action. How can we measure the success or failure of a concerted effort to change the world for the better? How and when do our attempts to improve the lot of others actually work? How is success in such moral and ethical endeavor to be defined? Stark's former naïve techno-faith may have proved inadequate in the face of these questions; but his sincere desire to "improve the world" clearly remains, for all that he is now unsure how to proceed.

Later events establish that Stark International no longer takes defense contracts, although Stark is under pressure from his board of directors to relax his opposition to this source of funding. He has responded by retreating into his workshop, where he tinkers with the Iron Man project, despite being increasingly uncertain of its purpose. He reacts to Pillinger's aggressive questioning in the same way, canceling his appointments for the day and retreating to the basement where the Iron Man suit stands at the ready in a launching tube. Speaking for a voice log, Stark wonders aloud whether Pillinger is right to regard Iron Man as a military device. The suit "is used for extraordinary rescue and response situations," he says, and once represented "the future" in his mind. But he admits having a more selfish reason for continuing to develop the project after first inventing it in Afghanistan, and even after subsequent heart surgery in the United States meant he was no longer dependent on the Iron Man chest plate to save his life. "It wasn't about *the* future, but *my* future . . . it allowed me to pretend that I wasn't a man who made landmines. I went from being a man trapped in an iron suit to being a man freed by it." Then, dressed as Iron Man, he launches himself into the sky, laughing with delight. (It is the only time Tony Stark laughs in the entire story.)

Ellis thus deftly telescopes events from the first two decades of the *Iron Man* comics of the 1960s and 1970s in order to explore the theme of misplaced techno-faith and its consequences. The Iron Man armor itself is portrayed as performing a dual and potentially contradictory psychological function for its creator. As a device designed for "extraordinary rescue and response" situations, it is an expression of Stark's guilty conscience over his past work as a weapons designer; but as a marvelous mechanical toy that raises his physical capabilities to superhuman levels it also serves him as a private source of emotional release. Although initially conceived for use as a "social" technology, then, the Iron Man is increasingly important to its creator as a technological crutch for his ego, which is otherwise crippled by self-loathing. But Ellis's Stark is also reflective enough to know this about himself, which is why when confronted by Pillinger (and later, by an old mentor) with the key question, "What's the Iron Man *for*?" he is unable to provide an answer. He has lost faith in his capacity to "improve the world" through technology, and with the collapse of that belief system he has become paralyzed—reduced to employing his greatest invention for temporarily liberating thrills, such as jet-powered flight.

The plot contrasts Stark with two other figures: Maya Hansen, a biotechnologist and old friend of Stark's; and Mallen, a domestic terrorist, and the childhood survivor of events that seem loosely based on the tragedy of Ruby Ridge in 1992 (when government officers killed the wife and child of alleged white separatist, Randy Weaver). Both these figures represent alternative attitudes toward the future that Stark once hoped to create. Hansen also wants to change the world through technological innovation, but she lacks Stark's scruples; she is happy to work for the military if it means achieving her goals as a researcher. With defense industry funds, she has invented Extremis, "a bio-electronics package fitted into a few billion graphic nanotubes and suspended in a carrier fluid" that "rewrite[s] the repair center of the brain" on injection—essentially hacking the operating system of the human body to transform the recipient into a super-soldier with devastating physical abilities. Mallen, on the other hand, wishes to "kill" the future, to "turn back the clock" to his idealized vision of the past, before America became a police state, when organizations like the Ku Klux Klan "defended Christian Law." He appreciates the irony of using a technology of the future to fight against it. Injecting himself with a stolen dose of Extremis, Mallen assaults an FBI building in Houston, Texas, killing as many as 50 government workers, before heading to Washington DC to do more damage.

When Iron Man first attempts to stop him, his armored suit proves no match for Mallen's biotechnical powers; his more old fashioned mechanical enhancements simply cannot respond quickly enough. Severely injured in this battle, Stark decides to reconfigure Extremis, with Hansen's help, into a form that will not only heal his wounds but also allow him to wire the Iron Man operating system directly into his brain—merging man with machine more completely than ever before. After this procedure, he is not only able control the armor by thought, "as if it were another limb," but also mentally access all forms of smart-tech—meaning that he can, for example, "see through satellites." Iron Man then fights Mallen for a second time; and in the course of this more evenly matched battle, the two men also argue over the value and purpose of the biotechnology that is the source of their powers. Mallen declares that he has "been given a tool to save people like me from those criminals in the White House." (It's one sign of the maturity of Ellis's writing that his supervillain does not cackle maniacally about ruling the world, but instead regards himself as the true hero of the piece.) Stark tells Mallen that he is just a "murder-happy hillbilly who never in his life had a thought about what these tools are for." The obvious implication is that the morality of technology cannot be considered apart from the morality of the user. He also tells Mallen that he has "spent years trying to get out of the arms race [and] make this suit into something that doesn't just kill." But Mallen forces his hand; their battle is to the death.

Unhappy in his victory, Stark then discovers that Maya Hansen deliberately leaked the Extremis sample to Mallen's militia in the first place, after the US army pulled funding for her project. When confronted, she argues that the end justifies the means: "I would have used the renewed funding to get out of the arms race. Set up on my own. Medical technology." She dismisses Mallen's victims in purely utilitarian terms as acceptable losses on the way to this goal: "More than 50 people die in car accidents every day." Her parting shot to Stark, as members of the security forces lead her away, is that "There's no difference between us, Tony. You're no better than me." She is referring, of course, to the fact that Stark's own inventions, including the Iron Man armor, are the fruits of his initial work as a manufacturer of weapons—weapons that we know from the Pillinger interview have maimed and killed innocents. Stark, still costumed as Iron Man, bows his head as if in acknowledgement that Hansen's words have struck home. But he straightens for the final image of the story—a full page portrait, posed heroically like a classical heroic bust, viewed from a dramatically low angle so that the reader looks up at him— and without denying Hansen's charge that he is "no better" than she, he tells her "But I'm trying to be. And I'm going to be able to look at myself in the mirror tomorrow morning."

Granov's imagery nicely complements Ellis's text here, by deploying familiar visual conventions that encourage us to buy into the notion of Tony Stark's essential nobility and goodness. But no amount of visual symbolism can disguise how battered and diminished this vision of the technologically enhanced hero really is. Ellis's story is built upon the proposition that it is easier to invent miraculous and innovative technologies than to arrive at a clear moral vision with regard to their use. Redesigning the human body from the inside out is apparently less of a challenge for his characters than answering the question of whether or why they should do so. One of the points most powerfully made by *Extremis*, then, is that it is hard to be a hero when basic ethics is more difficult than advanced science. Moral uncertainty and the acknowledgment of imperfection and failure are the only reliable indicators of "goodness" in this text. Thus, Stark spends most of the story unsure of the real purpose of the Iron Man suit he has invented, and John Pillinger is also marked as a good man precisely to the extent that he doesn't know what his journalistic work has achieved. By contrast, Mallen's moral absolutism is destructive, self-righteous, and terrifying, while Hansen's utilitarian logic is no less evil beneath its mask of cold, calculating "rationality."

It is tempting to read Mallen's false idealization of a nonexistent past, his racism, and his self-righteousness, and Hansen's self-serving techno-faith, as together representing the very worst excesses of liberal humanism, at least as that philosophy is portrayed in the writings of some postwar philosophers and literary scholars. But if this makes Ellis's Iron Man the representative of either an antihumanist or posthumanist alternative to "all-too-human" humanist values—a reading that is certainly encouraged by Stark's literal transformation into a posthuman amalgam of man and machine—it's still hard to say precisely what the content or intellectual assumptions of that alternative might be. As is also the case with many contemporary literary theorists and philosophers, it is easier to say what Ellis's Iron Man *doesn't* stand for—moral and intellectual absolutes—than what he does. Still, it attests to a widespread decline of faith in "Man" and his reason that the ethical standing of the superhero in this particular technological fantasy is defined less by his righteousness than by an anguished self-consciousness regarding his own moral failings, and a lack of confidence in the purpose of his considerable knowledge and power.

Also somewhat obscure, but no less intriguing, are the competing roles of alcoholism and recovery within this narrative. Ellis's Stark is more of a "recovered" alcoholic than Michelinie and Layton's "dry drunk." Unlike the character in *Armor Wars*, he is not wistful about drinking, but speaks of his former alcohol abuse dispassionately, and in the past tense. Maya Hansen, by contrast, is not only a drinker, but may actually be an alcoholic in denial. The hints are subtle—insufficient for a clear diagnosis—but they have a cumulative impact. For example, early in the story we discover that Hansen and Stark initially met in bar at a "Techwest" conference during his own drinking days. When she reestablishes contact with him she reminds him of the "lousy pub at Techwest" and the deal they made there to "always take each other's calls"—evoking their former bond as drinking buddies. In a later chapter, their mutual mentor, futurist Sal Kennedy, who was also at this Techwest gathering, recalls Maya rather than Tony as the one who "turned up drunk" for his talk. At another point, Hansen also asks Stark, apparently *apropos* of nothing, if he's "still not drinking," a question that in itself indicates a failure to understand the nature of alcoholism. Stark responds without elaboration or self-pity: "Don't dare. I'm an alcoholic." To which Hansen replies, somewhat insensitively, but also revealingly: "Jack Daniels is my boyfriend." It is possible to dismiss this remark as an ill-timed joke, but it's surely significant that Ellis includes this exchange at all; and if taken seriously, it implies that Hansen drinks alone, and regards alcohol as a substitute for emotional connections. Later still, when she is about to tell Stark what Extremis does, and why its theft is so devastating, she asks for a drink first, but Stark does not have one to offer her.

Given that Hansen is also reliant on defense contracts to develop Extremis—something else that Stark has renounced—it's hard not to see Ellis drawing a parallel between the dangers created by alcohol dependence and those created by a technological dependence on the economics of the military industrial complex. Likewise, we might also sense a connection being made between Hansen's alcoholic drinking and her callous pursuit of her own desires, regardless of the harm that results. Less obvious, but surely implied, is a connection between Stark's recovery from alcoholism and his repudiation of the rewards of defense work, and indeed, his more general effort to become a "better" person, in an explicitly moral and ethical sense. But questions remain: how can he pursue, define, or measure his own moral growth without falling back into a misguided self-righteousness? How can he do the right thing in a world where the only certainty is that he cannot be certain whether he is doing the right thing?

6

Let us gather up these various threads and start toward a conclusion. At first blush, it might seem that Tony Stark's dual careers—as a millionaire industrialist with a history of arms dealing on the one hand, and as a technologically enhanced super-warrior on the other—represent the triumph of the ideologies of capitalism and techno-faith over traditional religious values. Therefore, we might reasonably expect Iron Man to be the least "spiritual" of superheroes, and a curious object of study for a book of this kind. However, on closer examination, it turns out that many Iron Man stories reveal at their heart—quite literally, given the centrality of that organ to the earliest comics—a profound ambivalence toward the role of technology within modern society. More specifically, in many of the stories that I have considered (and there are others to which I could point), the relationship between technology and the capitalist military industrial complex is characterized as an unhealthy form of mutual dependence, one that ultimately limits creative possibility and moral growth. As different writers have explored this relationship within the series over the course of the last five decades, the slippage between empowerment and dependence that was always implicit in the origin of the character through the figure of his life-sustaining chest plate has only became more pronounced, even after the original injury to his heart was cured by surgery. Consequently, today, Iron-Man's technological enhancements do nothing so well as draw attention to the failings, needs, and weaknesses of Tony Stark, the man inside the magical suit. And significantly, those failings have generally turned out to be the result of what we might call misapplications of the will: that is, determined but misguided attempts to achieve conscious control over aspects of both the world and the self that are simply not amenable to such efforts. Tony Stark's painful struggles to "improve" himself and the world through technology thus end up bringing the reader back to a set of essentially spiritual questions about the nature of the self and the purpose of the will—albeit reconfigured within a recognizably contemporary world filled with prosthetic extensions and technological proxies for that self and will.

These, then, are some of the fundamentally spiritual questions underlying the dramatic conflicts of the *Iron Man* series: Do the possibilities of technology foster a dangerous faith in the unlimited potential of human reason? Does this dangerous techno-faith actually increase the suffering it hopes to mitigate? Does it encourage a form of self-destructive dependency, even in the pursuit of an impossible dream of absolute power? If so, how can we recover from this dependency? Can we hope to find rather than lose the self in the "other" of technology? Can we accept the notion that, however technologically extended the human will might become, its scope will always remain finite? Can we accept that limitation is a condition of any individual life—however ingenious and creative that individual may be? And if so, can we still hope to do good—despite the fact that our inherent, inescapable, human limitations make it hard even to know what "good" is?

I do not believe it is a coincidence that these questions, which are perhaps always implicit in any sophisticated techno-fantasy, become more pressing following the introduction of the theme of alcoholism to the series. For addiction is not just a powerful allegory for the experience and consequences of techno-dependency; instead, as I've already suggested, drugs and alcohol are themselves technologies, the abuse of which can be characterized by the effort to extend the human will into an area that is not its natural province—the area of emotional states and feelings.[30] Elaborating on this notion, the psychoanalyst Leslie H. Farber argued that the fundamental desire of the addict was for "a subjective experience of wholeness," that, once achieved through drugs or alcohol, left the user vulnerable to the belief

> . . . that the relief the drug afforded is an extraordinary sort of transcendence which his usual life with others cannot provide, except in the occasional unpredictable and surprising manner in which such moments arise. In other words, he has been burned by

the demonic and addictive notion that he need not wait on life for the transcendence he seeks, that he may invoke it whenever he so decrees or wills by returning to the drug or drugs that first allowed him this remarkable feeling.

With this seeming triumph of his will, he will be more impatient of the often frustrating give-and-take of life without drugs, willfully demanding his well-being of those about him and thereby suffering even more the penalties of such willing. In a sense he insists futilely that life now be his drug. Needless to say, his mounting impatience will be inimical to the exercise or development of such qualities as imagination, judgment, humor, tact. And should he glimpse, however dimly, his impoverishment, he may wish to believe these qualities at least can return with drugs, disowning the evidence accumulating to the contrary . . . As his intolerance for life without drugs increases, his competence for such life diminishes, so that with every return to the drug he is, in the spirit of Heraclitus, a different and lesser person who attempts to cross the same stream twice.[31]

Farber was not afraid to generalize from this powerful description of the individual addictive cycle. He went so far as to characterize our present era as "the Age of the Disordered Will" in which "every citizen is instructed by the public media that there is no portion of his life that is not wholly within his control."

If life is difficult for you, an evening of television watching will teach you how to dispel your miseries through aspirin, deodorants, mouthwash, dance lessons, laxatives, vitamins, hair lotions, and edifying panel programs. And more professional sources can provide tranquilizers, stimulants, psychoanalysis, sleeping pills, religion, or instruction in sexual technique and business relations.[32]

Thus, Farber ends his account of the individual addict's delusion with the following statement:

Nietzsche, I believe, was not as interested in theological arguments about the disappearance of the divine will in our lives as he was in the consequences of its disappearance. Today, the evidence is in. Out of disbelief we have impudently assumed that all of life is subject to our own will. And the disasters that have come from willing what cannot be willed have not at all brought us to some modesty about our presumptions.[33]

Farber was among the first and most eloquent writers of the twentieth century to suggest that the psychological study of addiction could provide insight into the fraught conditions of late modernity in general, with its endless multiplication of dubious technologies of the will. But in the wider context that Farber sketches, the question of "recovery" obviously takes on a new urgency. Might the treatment of substance abuse provide even those of us who are *not* addicted to alcohol or drugs with some new models or languages for addressing the problems of late modernity, and the attendant crisis of humanist techno-faith?

As is well known, most treatment programs for substance abuse—including Alcoholic Anonymous, the most popular and successful treatment for alcoholism worldwide—posit a "spiritual" solution to the individual alcoholic's dilemma. Unfortunately, the mere evocation of the spiritual is enough for some secular humanists to dismiss the suggestion AA "works" at all (and to insist, if it does, it's not in the way that the intellectually naïve members of the fellowship think). The suggestion that the culture at large might benefit from an infusion of the philosophy of recovery will therefore undoubtedly be received with incredulity and even sputters of indignation from certain quarters. But actually the precise nature of the "spirituality" advocated by the 12-step programs is generally very poorly understood, even within contemporary academic theological schools.[34] For example, it is sometimes mistakenly characterized as a form of dogmatic Christian evangelism, in which the drinker substitutes his or her addiction to alcohol for an addiction to religion. This assessment is understandable, given the frequent repetition of the word "God" in those famous 12 Steps, the broadly Protestant origins of the founding members, and the practice, common during the earliest days of the program, of ending meetings with a recitation of the Lord's Prayer. The fact that many other "temperance" movements, both before and since the establishment of AA, adopt the principle that the alcoholic must be "saved" according to a particular—usually Christian—understanding of that term has further added to the evangelical reputation of the AA fellowship.

But the theological character of AA is in fact less dogmatic and more apophatic than this; far from being a throwback to a premodern form of religiosity it instead anticipates a mode of thought that some contemporary philosophers are nowadays trying to catch at through such concepts as "the post-secular," or even more deliberately paradoxical formulations, such as "religion without religion."[35] At the same time, AA advocates an imminently practical, almost antitheoretical spirituality, to the extent that it negotiates some of the more familiar swamps of theological debate by branding certain topics (such as, say, the actual qualities of God, or the nature of morality) as "outside issues"—that is, questions than an individual is encouraged to ponder, but about which AA has no official position.

As historian Ernest Kurtz has noted in his invaluable and detailed study of the intellectual origins of AA, the foremost spiritual principle of the program is not that salvation will be found when the alcoholic acknowledges God, but rather that relief depends upon the alcoholic acknowledging that he or she is *not* God.[36] Since even the worst alcoholic or drug addict is not usually so narcissistically damaged as to admit, even to him or herself, that he or she aspires to the condition of the deity, it may be hard to see why this principle is so important, at first. But if we recall Farber's account of the psychological trajectory of the addictive process, this emphasis on what Kurtz calls "not-God-ness" may start to make more sense; because whatever the conscious motivation of the addict—pain, anxiety, shyness, loneliness, or even an excess of joy, as in the celebratory drink that goes horribly wrong—whatever the conscious motive, the point is that the addict refuses to "wait on life" for the experience of transcendence, instead deploying a technology in order to attain the emotional state that he or she desires, when he or she desires it. Or as Kurtz puts it, "the alcoholic, in drinking, . . . sought inappropriate control over reality—more [power] than was granted to human finitude."[37] According to the philosophy of AA, as Kurtz makes clear, this bid for "autonomous self-determination of moods and feelings" involves "a claim to unlimitedness, . . . a claim beyond any human," and so "a claim to the absolute."[38] It is also in the context of this effort to will what cannot be willed that we should read the words of Bill Wilson in AA's Big Book: "First of all we had to quit playing God."[39]

To be clear: The point is *not* that all alcoholics are self-regarding narcissists. Insofar as it is self-centered to want to control one's feelings at all times, then Wilson and AA do find the alcoholic guilty as charged; but they do not assume that this kind of self-centeredness is the same thing as narcissistic grandiosity. In fact, just the opposite condition—self-hatred—may be equally likely to fuel the self-centered desire to "play God," in Wilson's sense of the phrase. Hence the witty and paradoxical formulations that have become familiar jokes within the literature of the program, such as the statement that "an alcoholic is an ego-maniac with an inferiority complex," or the more personally self-deprecating "I'm not much, but I'm all I think about."

Of course, one might respond that it is perfectly possible to recognize that one is not God without committing to the position that there is therefore a "Higher Power" out there for the alcoholic to rely upon. But as Kurtz points out, this position is regarded as something of a bad sign within AA:

But once . . . the alcoholic has accepted this truth [of his not-Godness], AA occasionally faced a new problem with its newly sober member . . . yes, he was not God, but that was all right because there was no God—no absolute—anyway. This equivalent denial of *any* ultimate reality . . . still implied the ultimate self-centeredness that Alcoholics Anonymous had diagnosed as the root of the alcoholic's problem.[40]

First of all, we should note that "God" here has ceased to be a benevolent metaphysical being imbued with omniscience and omnipotence, and has become something rather more abstract—a (non) being who, by His absence suggests the (non)existence of absolutes. At this point, it is almost as if the alcoholic of Kurtz's example has become a neo-pragmatist philosopher, denying the necessity of foundations, or a postmodernist denying the existence of a God as a transcendent signifier. The response Kurtz attributes to AA is also curiously like that of a number of critics of postmodern thought: concern that this denial of the existence of an "ultimate reality" will lead to a damaging solipsism.

I do not propose to try to settle the vexed question of whether philosophical anti-foundationalism—perhaps the most sophisticated version of the position adopted here by Kurtz's alcoholic—entails a logical commitment to solipsism. I am not even sure that particular issue *can* be settled, given the apparently interminable nature of the argument within academic philosophy departments. Instead, I simply want to emphasize the perhaps unexpected way in which the theology of Alcoholic Anonymous assumes that, in the absence of God, Man cannot help but put himself in the former place of the deity, taking on his prerogatives—with potentially disastrous consequences. (To this extent, the AA position is perhaps closer to the philosophy of Nietzsche than has been previously realized.)

Kurtz then goes on to describe the response of AA to the alcoholic's denial of an "ultimate reality."

> AA argued neither philosophy nor theology, but rather pointed to the simple fact in the drinker's experience . . . The alcoholic had been unable to stop his drinking, the obsessive compulsive acting out of alcoholism, on his own, by himself. . . . The first steps did not require classic belief in a traditional "God"; but they did require the alcoholic to accept his not-God-ness by acknowledging *some* "Power greater" than himself. The AA group itself, clearly, was such a "Higher Power." Its members had achieved what he could not, and in that admission lay the true core of the alcoholic's acceptance of not-God-ness: there was some Higher Power; there did actually exist a power greater than his own.
>
> Such acknowledgment was surely attenuated infinity and but small transcendence, yet it made the point. . . . The very existence of the AA group as successfully sober not only taught but riveted attention on these two truths: the individual alcoholic was hopelessly limited, and he could transcend that limitation only by reaching beyond himself to others.[41]

Again, the point is *not* that the alcoholic should regard the sober members of AA as God's representatives on Earth; if that were the case AA would indeed be the cult that some have accused it of being. The point is rather that the sober members of AA have achieved something together that they could not manage alone; thus, collectively, each recovered alcoholic has found "a power greater than himself [or herself]"—a power greater than that which he or she wielded as an individual. They have learned, as Beth Cabe tells Tony Stark in the final pages of the *Demon in a Bottle* story arc, to "stop playing the . . . loner and share" the burden of their lives. The logic could not be simpler; if you can't admit that there may be powers greater than your own in the world, then you can't be helped by those powers. To refuse this admittedly "attenuated," less-than-metaphysical notion of "Higher Power"—which, presumably, one does not even have to find in an AA group, as long as one finds it somewhere—would clearly be to isolate oneself profoundly.

But if refusal of the notion of a power greater than the self in this most moderate sense implies isolation, what does it mean to *accept* it? To accept it is to accept in a no less profound way the truth of one's personal weakness, limitation, and need. The choice as presented, then, is isolation, but with the comforting illusion of omnipotence, or fellowship, based on an acknowledgment that some things—perhaps many things—are forever beyond the reach of our control. It should be obvious that it is not just individuals that make the first choice; it is possible to understand many of the more tragic political decisions of the last century or so in terms of the pursuit of the illusion of omnipotence, at the cost of isolation.

AA does not so much posit the existence of any particular God, then, but rather insists on the necessity of the God concept, as a means of preserving an enabling human humility (two words that share the same root in the notion of being "of the earth"). Alive to paradox, it is a theology that could be described as both pietistic—or even antihumanist—and humanist at once. Thus, the traditional binary opposition of God/Man, when rewritten as an opposition between God/not-God, becomes a hedge against humanist arrogance, and perhaps even against the temptations of binary thought in general (since this is not strictly speaking an opposition at all, but more a foundational negation). But this pietistic antihumanism is combined with an emphasis on the blessing of human fellowship; moreover, it is conceived as the essential path to that fellowship, which is itself based not so much upon a positively defined notion of "shared humanity," but rather upon a shared insufficiency, a common mutual need.

In the last 50 years—about the period since Iron Man first entered the scene of pop culture, in fact—it has become increasingly common for some intellectuals to condemn the failings of a loosely defined "humanism," and for others to point out that such critiques are invariably performed in the name of what are "unmistakable humanist, even Enlightenment, ends of understanding and emancipation."[42] But, in their not-quite separate ways, the Iron Man comics and the philosophy of AA can serve to remind us that these complex philosophical debates are at bottom prompted by the effort to address some basic but difficult questions about the nature and limits of human agency. Just how much can human beings affect their own destiny and that of the planet? What, finally, are the limits of the human will?

Thinkers who stress the role and responsibility of the autonomous individual (a position associated with the Enlightenment traditions of liberalism and humanism) inevitably run up against the charge that they overlook the enormous role played by social, political, and even biological factors in determining human behavior. Thinkers who stress the constructed, partial, and mediated nature of the self, the problematic role of the unconscious, and the historical contingency that undermines all attempts to characterize a "universal" human nature (positions associated with late modernist and postmodern thought) inevitably run up against the charge that they do not offer a coherent account of human freedom, and provide no foundation for morality outside of a relativistic pragmatism. Extreme versions of either position tend to strike most of us as inherently unsatisfactory, but it is difficult to thread a path between them without courting considerable complexity—or at least a measure of self-conscious paradox. Without pretending that a simple resolution is possible or even desirable, I would like to suggest that the "attenuated" spirituality of AA is just such a complex and paradoxical response to the apparent impasse of humanist and antihumanist thought, in its insistence that the acknowledgment of the limits of human power must be the first step toward the taking of collective responsibility to address human needs.

Whether one finds this response persuasive or convincing is another matter entirely. But even if you do not think we need the concept of "a power greater than ourselves" in order to rediscover the fact of human neediness and vulnerability, and hence to rediscover the joy—and the power—of fellowship and collective action, there can be no doubt that this essential human neediness is more masked than alleviated by our proliferating technologies of the will. To put it another way, Tony Stark's abiding need for others is the repressed kernel of truth that underwrites his—and our—investment in the technological fantasy of radical independence, invulnerability, and perfection that he otherwise embodies. That is why he acknowledges that need so reluctantly, and why those moments of acknowledgment, when they come, carry the emotional weight that they do. Tony's profound need is what makes it possible for me to describe the scene from the first *Iron Man* movie with which I began as a sex scene; with its portrayal of embarrassed good humor, awkward desire, frank affection, and honest communication, it stands as the most genuine moment of intimacy in the entire film. The message of that emblematic moment is therefore also the message of Iron Man's most enduring comic book adventures: technology might save your skin, but if you really want to heal your heart, you have to admit your vulnerability, acknowledge your basic need, take off your armor—and reach out.

CODA: MODERN GODS

The American comic book superhero has obvious antecedents in ancient Greek, Norse, and Afroasiatic literatures. But Superman, Wonder Woman, Spider-Man, Iron Man, and their many compatriots are also fantasy figures that negotiate such modern phenomena as the rise of science, the decline of traditional structures of religion, the processes of industrialization and urbanization, the pressures of nationalism, and the effects of capitalism. They are not nomadic, country-roving warriors, but city-dwelling heroes, with powers and tools and "secret identities" that arise in specific response to the cramped and crowded conditions of metropolitan existence.[1] Their abilities are generally not supernatural in origin, but are explained by appeals to science and technology (even Marston's *Wonder Woman*, a strip in which the Olympian Gods at times play a direct and active role, stresses the superiority of "Amazon science"). They not only identify with the political culture and goals of the United States of America, but are also capable of acknowledging that they inhabit a class system, and sometimes articulate an explicitly social account of ethics (as the analysis of Superman's adventures of the late 1930s in my first chapter makes clear). All of these factors set American comic book superheroes apart from more traditional mythic heroes.

As fantasy hybrids that draw upon premodern tropes but place them in a distinctly modern context, superhero comics can expose some of the unacknowledged contradictions of modernity itself, if we put the right questions to them. And although I have not written the book that I think still needs to be written about "superheroes and modernity," I hope my attention here to the nondenominational spirituality of the superhero fantasy may serve as something of an initial contribution to such a project. For example, one of the things that

I hope this study suggests is the ultimate falsehood of the characteristically modern oppositions between religion and science, or deism and humanism. I dealt with this topic most directly in my final chapter, on Iron Man, but it is obviously implicit in the basic notion of a fantasy about distinctly modern men (and women) who possess the powers of the gods.

Superheroes do not render sacred concepts in secular terms for a skeptical modern audience, as is sometimes claimed. They do something more interesting; they deconstruct the oppositions between sacred and secular, religion and science, god and man, the infinite and the finite, by means of an impossible synthesis. They are therefore fantasy solutions to some of the central dichotomies of modernity itself. A cynic might conclude that the suspension of disbelief required to enjoy such fantasies applies no less to their unlikely depictions of ethical perfection as it does to the spectacle of men and women who can fly, climb walls, and see through the satellites. But, less cynically, we might instead interpret these stories as testaments to the strength of not just our will-to-power, but also of our will-to-love—our will-to-kindness, concern, and decency. The dream of the superhero is not just a dream of flying, not just a dream about men and women who wield the powers of the gods. It's also a dream about men and women who never give up the struggle to be good. W. B. Yeats once wrote, "in dreams begin responsibilities." But perhaps possibilities of all kinds begin in dreams. And perhaps among these possibilities there is still the prospect of a spiritual awakening— even from within the skeptical, rationalist, materialist assumptions of modernity.

ON THE PLACE OF SUPERHERO STUDIES
WITHIN COMICS STUDIES

This is an exciting time for those of us who love the art of comics. Once casually disparaged and denigrated by critics and educators alike, the form is now more highly regarded within our institutions of art and culture. Well-researched histories and insightful critical analyses can be found on almost every aspect of comic book culture in North America; newspaper strips, underground and alternative comics, comic books, and graphic novels have all received a respectful reevaluation. Several academic journals devoted to the scholarly study of comics have launched in the last 10 years, including the University of Florida's frequently wonderful *ImageTexT*, and most recently, David Huxley and Joan Ormrod's *Journal of Graphic Novels and Comics*. There's room for more comparative criticism; but book-length studies on key aspects of British, Russian, and Indian comic history have all appeared in the last few years, and the already extensive bibliography on manga keeps growing.[1] And while cool elective classes on comics have been offered by universities across the United States since the 1970s, in the last decade or so if has finally started to seem that Comics Studies might bloom into a fully-fledged academic discipline—within which students could take several different comics related courses, exploring the sequential art of different cultures and time periods, reading key creators in more depth, and experimenting with their own creative work.[2] Some important questions must be debated as we make our way toward this desirable goal, however, and I want to consider just a few of them here, and perhaps sound a cautionary note with regard to some possible missteps along the way. As will rapidly become clear, these questions have an immediate urgency for me, as the author of a study that takes superhero comics for its subject; but I hope their relevance to the wider community of comics scholars will also be apparent.

It seems to me that two key dangers can arise as we enter into discussions about how to organize the content of our Comics Studies courses. One is that of uncritically importing value judgments and historical assumptions from fan-culture, without subjecting them to skeptical scrutiny.[3] I include as part of fan-culture the claims made by influential practitioner-theorists of the form such as Will Eisner, Scott McCloud, and Art Spiegelman. (Hearing the history of comics from Art Spiegelman is a little like hearing the history of poetry from T. S. Eliot; few people could teach you more about the subject, and few could be more tendentious in their views.) As scholars, we will have to question critical narratives that, in our guise as fans, we may have learned to cherish. Speaking personally, I can sometimes find this transition from fan to scholar difficult—I've been mildly obsessed with comic books since I was six years old, after all, which makes it difficult to achieve "critical distance"—and some readers will already have identified ways in which I have failed to make the leap in my work. But that is one of the reasons we have intellectual communities; so that we can strengthen our scholarly narratives collectively, thereby deepening our knowledge and understanding in ways that we could not do alone. To this extent—while no one likes to be told they have got something wrong—I welcome the corrective arguments of my fellow scholars, as signs of the growing health of Comics Studies as a discipline.

The second and perhaps greater danger is the possibility of a critical division emerging between comics scholars along lines that replicate the most basic opposition of current American comic book culture: that is, the opposition between those who mostly consume serialized genre fictions (largely dominated by but *not* limited to superhero stories, often but *not* only published by one of the corporate owned houses of Marvel and DC) and those who mostly consume the work of independent creators specializing in what we might call "comics-lit" (largely dominated by but *not* limited to the nonfiction genres of autobiography and documentary). Metonymically, we might think of this in creator terms as the "Bendis versus Bechdel" argument, or, in terms of famous comic convention sites, as Wondercon versus Stumptown. (There are, of course, many creators and readers out there who enjoy material from both sides of this putative divide— I count myself as one of them—but just as with music and movies, there are consumers and critics who are more partisan in their tastes.)

It is all-too-easy for the old-fashioned binaries of high culture versus low culture, fine art versus commercial art, and "alternative" versus "mainstream," to reassert themselves along the lines of this division. (Despite the best efforts of literary theorists to deconstruct such aesthetic hierarchies, they prove remarkably resilient; with almost tragic irony, they frequently reproduce themselves within the critical subcultures that emerge around art forms undervalued within conservative aesthetic circles.)[4] In fact, for quite some time it has been possible to detect this replication of traditional aesthetic hierarchies—in which genre comics in general, and superhero comics in particular, are regarded with aesthetic suspicion—in some of our most important vehicles of comics criticism. For example, in 1999, when contributors to *The Comics Journal* first attempted to generate a "comics canon"—a list of 100 of the most significant comic-art creations of the twentieth century—genre works were mostly excluded. The absence of superhero comics from the list was particularly striking; even applying the broadest generic definition, only four examples cracked the *Journal*'s top 50: Will Eisner's *The Spirit*, at #15; Lee and Kirby's *Fantastic Four*, at #30; Jack Cole's *Plastic Man*, at #32; and Lee and Ditko's *Amazing Spider-Man*, at #35. Superman, Batman, and Wonder Woman—three of the most recognizable comic book icons in the world—were not represented by a *single* story.[5] Even in the notoriously subjective realm of aesthetic judgment, these are omissions that require explanation. I suspect there's more than one cause, and I'd like to consider a few possibilities.

First, the hostility of certain comics scholars toward superheroes might be partly accounted for as a reaction to the common tendency among casual observers to conflate the entire form with this single popular genre. It is a fact that the phrase "comic book" evokes visions of costumed crime fighters in the minds of many people; and when comics critics see the richly expressive and generically diverse history of their beloved medium reduced to this single category, it's understandable that they get frustrated. (Imagine trying to talk about the cinema with a person whose idea of the movies is limited to a handful of Westerns, and you'll get some idea of how this feels.)

Second, the political self-consciousness of much professional academic criticism since the 1970s—the generally salutary awareness that aesthetic questions do not stand apart from social and political ones—may also have contributed to the aversion to superheroes expressed by some comics scholars. The commonplace assumption that superhero comics are really just crude fantasies of power and domination licenses superficial dismissal from certain critics who imagine themselves on the left (despite their obvious discomfort with popular culture). Thus, for example, John Shelton Lawrence and Robert Jewett argue in *The Myth of the American Superhero* (2002) that superhero fantasies encourage an oversimplified and antidemocractic response to real-world problems and conflicts—fostering the illusion that complex geopolitical situations can be resolved by the international equivalent of a punch in the jaw. These two professors would have you believe that there is a direct relationship between the disastrous foreign policies pursued by the Bush administration after the events of 9/11 and the American national fascination with popular heroes like Superman and Spider-Man. But such provocative claims are hard to sustain when one examines the actual content of the comics that first gave us these characters.[6] Instead, as I have tried to show in my own work, comics creators have long been conscious of the contradiction between the will-to-power and the will-to-good expressed in the basic superhero fantasy, and have frequently exploited that tension to great aesthetic and dramatic effect.

Third, there seems to be something of a double standard within Cultural Studies when it comes critical analyses of the kinds of popular culture that tend to be consumed by men and the kinds that tend to be consumed by women. As Jeffrey A. Brown has noted: "Feminist . . . research on media audiences has repeatedly justified women's pleasure in relation to such traditional 'female' genres . . . as soap operas and romantic fiction by illustrating the various ways that . . . [women] use the texts to understand and counter the female position within a misogynistic culture." But, "where female pleasures in media use have been validated, there has been . . . a parallel invalidation of male pleasures." Brown does "not think that . . . the feminist based research on audiences [was] meant to reduce gendered media use to the level of *women as active resisters* and *men as complicit dupes*," but he believes that "there has been a tendency for the overall understanding of audiences to drift into this sort of essentialism."[7] We should therefore perhaps be skeptical when we are told by one set of critics that stereotypically "female" popular entertainments and practices (such as reading romance novels, or posing nude on hipster websites) actually subvert patriarchal power structures, while being told by another that more traditionally "male" entertainments and practices (such as reading adventure stories or playing "violent" video games) reaffirm masculinist-fascist hegemony. And since superhero fantasies are often caricatured as "for boys only," the growth of Cultural Studies—something that we might have naively hoped would heighten appreciation of superhero comics and their creators—may actually have initially contributed to their ongoing critical devaluation.[8]

Finally, there's the fact that different interpretive communities "naturally" value different aspects of a given art form for different reasons, while simultaneously presuming that their own particular evaluative criteria are all that really counts. Thus, academic lit-crit types favor works of graphic memoir and autobiography—Allison Bechdel, Lynda Barry, Marjane Satrapi, and Art Spiegelman are among their touchstone creators—and this bias obviously reflects the many years they have spent in graduate school theorizing about "representations of the self," and attendant issues.[9] Fans of monthly genre comics, by contrast, tend to prize vividly kinetic art (among other things), with a preference for the techniques of a highly detailed "realism"; indeed, these fans often misrecognize more expressionistic styles as "bad" drawing. Meanwhile *The Comics Journal*, the longest running vehicle for quality comics criticism and an immensely important publication, stakes out some different aesthetic ground (though perhaps not a middle ground). While less swayed by the vagaries of academic fashion, and overtly receptive to all aspects of the comics form—featuring in-depth interviews with genre creators side-by-side with essays on "high-art" comics creators, European comics, and manga, for example—one may still detect a preference for the great comics auteurs in its pages (Caniff, Crane, Crumb, Foster, Los Bros. Hernandez, Segar, Schulz, *et al*), and a concomitant mistrust for the monthly "product" from the corporate publishing houses of Marvel and DC, which tends to be the work of multiple hands. (In fact, the superhero comics in the *Journal* top 50 are all readily intelligible in terms of the "auteurist" visions of Eisner, Kirby, Cole, and Ditko, even when other creators were involved in the process.)[10]

My point is not that we should be striving for a "value free" critical discourse—value free criticism is surely a contradiction in terms—but simply that as comics critics we may need to become more self-reflexive with regard to the aesthetic criteria of the interpretive community with which we most strongly identify, and to recognize that "our" preferred criteria are hardly the only ones. Because whatever the origins of the current critical divide between advocates of "art" comics and advocates of genre comics, it is surely unfortunate. To partisans of alternative and independent creators, I would therefore ask them to consider how likely it is that we will elevate the cultural status of the comics medium by ignoring and even denigrating some of its most successful creations? After all, when we talk about comic book superheroes we are talking about some of the most instantly recognizable and enduring fantasy figures to have emerged from the maelstrom of twentieth-century mass culture. As popular icons, Superman, Batman, and Wonder Woman are up there with Elvis Presley, James Dean, and Marilyn Monroe—and what's more, they show every sign of outpacing all three of their real world rivals in terms of ongoing significance. But besides the obvious fact of their cultural visibility, superhero comics have also contributed enormously to the *aesthetic* development of the comic book form—and not only by inspiring many an "alternative" creator to first pick up a pen—but for the reasons I have enumerated above, these formal and aesthetic achievements remain overlooked and poorly understood in our criticism. If as comics scholars we want to continue to raise appreciation and awareness of the art form, then it would seem sensible both to acknowledge the broad appeal of superheroes, and to encourage critical work that deepens our understanding of that appeal—in formal and aesthetic terms as well as psychological and social terms—rather than to regard superhero comics with sniffy disdain, as if they were a shameful blot upon the otherwise immaculate landscape of contemporary sequential art.

Of course, this is not to suggest that superheroes have been entirely ignored by the critics. Far from it; recent years have seen the publication of a number of book-length studies, employing a broad variety of hermeneutic strategies. Besides the mythological criticism and works of cultural studies that I have already noted, there have been structuralist accounts such as Peter Coogan's *Superhero: The Secret Origins of a Genre* (2006); psychologistic investigations of the "meaning" of superhero fantasies such as Danny Fingeroth's *Superman on the Couch* (2004) and Robin Rosenberg's anthology, *The Psychology of Superheroes* (2008); cultural histories on the origins of the comic book form, such as Gerard Jones's *Men of Tomorrow* (2004); engagingly written feminist discussions such as Lillian S. Robinson's *Wonder Women: Feminisms and Superheroes* (2004);

several books on superheroes and Judaism; and almost as many again devoted to exfoliating the philosophical, cultural, and sexual significations of Batman.[11] There have also been wide ranging anthologies, such as Angela Ndalianis's *The Contemporary Comic Book Superhero* (2009). But with one or two notable exceptions, and despite the methodological range of these analyses, "superhero studies" has not been noted for close attention to matters of aesthetic and formalist theory.

Critical partisans of the superhero genre, then, have something to learn from the best "alternative comics" criticism, as practiced by such fine writers as Bart Beaty, Charles Hatfield, Gene Kannenberg, Jr, Joseph Witek, and several others—all of whom display an acute sensitivity to the formal questions that most superhero scholars seem to forget.[12] Again, the reasons for this critical blind spot are complex and multiple. For example, the chilling effect created by the looming threat of litigation for copyright violation has probably inhibited such work; it is hard to engage in the sustained formal analysis of superhero comics when one's university or "small press" publisher is reluctant to include the relevant images—howsoever they may fall within provisions of fair-use—for fear of being sued by a large and wealthy corporation. But perhaps it is also because superhero comics particularly invite psychologistic and allegorical forms of interpretation (something that Douglas Wolk has noted in a strong essay on the subject) that many analysts of the genre (myself included) have found themselves focusing more on issues of character and narrative than on issues of visual style and storytelling.[13] The upshot is that discussions of the semiotics of the superhero genre, its particular approach to the hybridization of word and image, its dominant conventions with regard to panel-to-panel transitions—its *visuality*, in short—are rare within superhero studies, at least to date.[14]

But if, for complex reasons, a relative inattention to issues of formalist theory mars a good deal of the published work in superhero studies—including, I regret to say, my own work in the foregoing pages—that does not mean that we should dismiss superhero comics, or genre work in general, as inherently weaker than more academically fashionable works of graphic memoir and autobiography.[15] Instead, as I have tried to argue both explicitly and implicitly in the essays gathered in this small collection, the wish-fulfilling dreams of impossible strength, intelligence, vitality, and beauty that make up the primary material of superhero comics are not a cause for embarrassment, but one of the reasons they are so worthy of our attention. Rather than flatter ourselves that we are above such dreams of power and perfection, it would perhaps be more critically productive for us to own these dreams—to admit that they are sometimes ours, too. In this way, we can come to recognize that superhero stories appeal to so many people in part because in the guise of the superhuman power fantasy they express desires and aspirations that are thoroughly and even ordinarily human.

If these arguments have even half persuaded you, I hope you might also be persuaded that it will be better for the future of Comics Studies if we refuse to transform generic distinctions into hierarchical ones. We don't need to have our own version of the fight that some music critics got into back in the 1970s over the merits of rock versus disco (or that a rather earlier generation of literary critics got into over the merits of poetry versus the novel). The discipline we want to create together can surely be big enough to contain appreciative studies of "the spirituality of the superhero," shall we say, alongside accounts of "representations of the self in graphic memoir." What's more, it should be able to welcome and nurture scholars who want to do either or even both kinds of work—or to work on science-fiction comics of the 1950s, or to theorize the anthropomorphic visual codes of funny animal comics, or to think about how gender is represented in certain manga, or indeed, to write intelligent criticism about any aspect of this potentially limitless subject. The more broadly we conceive the project of Comics Studies, the clearer it becomes that we are talking about a field that extends far beyond the knowledge-horizon of any individual critic or creator, no matter how well informed. To put it more collaboratively: as comics scholars, we need each other. We need the broader community of an established academic discipline to do the work that remains in charting the achievements of the art form that so captivates us—and there is a lot of work to be done. Despite the good news with which I began, from the point of view of our institutions of culture and education, the art of comics remains the most theoretically neglected and undervalued system of representation that human beings have devised. I want to see this situation change decisively in my lifetime, and if you have made it this far, you probably like that idea, too. Let's get there, together.

Excelsior!

NOTES

INTRODUCTION

1 Alan Moore and Alan Davies, "Marvelman: Blue Murder," *Warrior Magazine* #8, (December, 1982), p. 4. The character is also known as Miracleman in the United States, due to litigation initiated by Marvel Comics. (Marvel succeeded in forcing the name change, and also in permanently alienating Alan Moore, the single most influential comic book writer of the next two decades. This bafflingly small-minded action therefore cost them millions in potential revenue.)

2 On the superheroic body, and the resonance of the imagery of flight in superhero comics, see Scott Bukatman's lyrical criticism in *Matters of Gravity* (Durham and London: Duke University Press, 2003).

3 With apologies to Stan Lee, the greatest alliterative poet of the genre.

4 Susan Neiman, *Evil In Modern Thought: An Alternative History of Philosophy* (Princeton and Oxford: Princeton University Press, 2002), p. 102.

5 Ibid., p. 5.

6 Here, I'm echoing and developing some perspicacious remarks by Douglas Wolk, in "Superheroes and Superreaders," *Reading Comics* (New York: Da Capo Press, 2007), p. 92: "Superhero comics . . . provide bold metaphors for discussing ideas or reifying abstractions into narrative fiction. They're the closest thing that exists right now to the 'novel of ideas.'"

7 Neiman, *Evil*, p. 7.

8 To some, this may sound like an assault upon the notion of reason; but unless you are inclined to undervalue the imagination, there is no need to hear it that way.

9 The concepts of the "Golden Age," "Silver Age," et al, have currency within fan culture, although there is disagreement about when precisely they begin and end. But roughly speaking, the Golden Age might be said to start with Superman's debut and to end with the first significant industry implosion: that is, 1938–1954. The Silver Age is sometimes seen as beginning with DC's resurrection of the Flash in 1956, but is mostly associated with the rise of Marvel Comics in the 1960s; agreement over when it came to an end is even less clear, but most fans would say no later than the early 1970s.

With some reservations, I have continued to deploy these terms in my work on superheroes because I believe it is reasonable—or at least defensible—to see the first thirty-five years or so of the superhero genre as made up of two more-or-less distinct historical periods, marked by recognizably different artistic conventions, with the shift occurring at some point in the mid 1950s. Some fans also speak of a "Bronze Age," a "Copper Age," and so on, but these categories describe shifts in the commercial value and collectability of comic books more than any real changes in comic book form and content. Even the concepts of the "Golden" and "Silver" ages tell us little about the development of other forms and genres, beyond the superhero, and when it comes to efforts to periodize comics history in a broader way, they may be more misleading than informative. It is possible that a future generation of comics scholars may decide to refine or even abandon these categories. (See 172n3.)

10 See my second chapter on Wonder Woman.
11 John D. Caputo, *On Religion* (London and New York: Routledge, 2001), pp. 59–60, 63.
12 Slavoj Žižek, *The Monstrosity of Christ* (Cambridge and London: The MIT Press, 2009), p. 259.
13 Ibid., p.256, 259.
14 Ibid., p. 258.
15 George Herbert, "The Reprisal," in *The Complete English Poems*, ed. John Tobin (London: Penguin Books, 2004), p. 33.
16 Although Caputo elsewhere enrolls Kierkegaard as one of his prophets, I think that the fiery-ironist mocker of "soft" theology would call Caputo an atheist. Nietzsche would be less kind. Of course, Caputo surely knows this too, which might make his appropriation of these figures clever and audacious, or misleading and hypocritical, depending on your perspective.
17 The most influential modern reading of Kierkegaard as advocating an essentially "irrational" conception of ethics is that of Alasdair MacIntyre, in *After Virtue* (Notre Dame: University of Notre Dame Press, 1981), pp. 38–43. Of course, MacIntyre believes that virtue can and must be squared with the rational, and therefore that his diagnosis of Kierkegaard's "irrationalism" is also a critique; but surely Kierkegaard's argument is that when it comes to true knowledge of God's will, rationality is not so much inadequate as beside the point? For a series of detailed expositions of this debate, including a piece by MacIntyre himself, see the essays in *Kierkegaard After MacIntyre*, eds. John J. Davenport and Anthony Rudd (Chicago and La Salle: Open Court Publishing Company, 2001).
18 I do not have the space—or the production budget—to address the question of whether and how the specifically graphic nature of superhero comics contributes to the performance of this task, but it surely does. A comparative study comparing the imagery of superhero comics with the traditions of religious iconography would be a welcome addition to the bibliography of superhero studies.

CHAPTER ONE

1 The first writer to explore the Superman-Christ parallel was probably John T. Galloway, Jr., in his proselytizing text, *The Gospel According To Superman* (Philadelphia and New York: J. P. Lippincott, 1973); Greg Garrett taps a similar vein in *Holy Superheroes! Exploring Faith and Spirituality in Comic Books* (Colorado Springs, CO: Pinon Press, 2005), as does Ken Schenck in "Superman: A Popular Culture Messiah," in *The Gospel According To Superheroes*, ed. B. J. Oropeza, (New York: Peter Lang, 2005), 33–49. Danny Fingeroth makes a bid for Moses over Jesus (while acknowledging the traditional Christian typological reading the unites both Biblical figures) in *Disguised As Clark Kent: Jews, Comics, and the Creation of the Superhero* (New York and London: Continuum, 2007), 44–45. Don LoCicero's *Superheroes and Gods: A Comparative Study from Babylonia to Batman* (Jefferson, NC, and London: McFarland and Co., 2008), 162–167, suggests several other mythical cousins for the Man of Steel; and a simple Google search, pairing "Superman" with any one of these religious or mythical figures, yields many results—mostly derivative, but some interestingly tendentious.

2 Jean-Luc Marion, *God Without Being* (Chicago and London: The University of Chicago Press, 1991), 12.

3 The great exception here is "Must There Be a Superman," from *Superman* #247 (Jan. 1972) by Elliot Maggin and Curt Swan; I discuss it elsewhere in this essay.

4 Socrates most famously equates the Beautiful with the Good in Plato's *Symposium*; but even the less mystically minded Aristotle claims that when a man acts virtuously, it is for the sake of "*kalon*"—a Greek term that can mean "beautiful," "noble," or "fine." (See, for example his *Nicomachean Ethics*, 1120a, 23–4.) In this vision, a genuinely ethical act has a formal balance or harmony analogous to that of a well-crafted artwork.

5 Dennis O'Neil, "The Man of Steel and Me," in *Superman at Fifty*, eds. Dennis Dooley and Gary Engle, (New York: MacMillan Collier Books, 1988), 51.

6 All these stories can be found in the invaluable collection, *The Superman Chronicles, Volume One* (New York: DC Comics, 2006), which reprints the first year of the character's adventures, from *Action Comics* #1 to *Superman* #1, in chronological order.

7 "Rousseau's brilliant . . . sociological insight into the divisive nature of modern society is scarcely coherent with his assertions . . . of the power and universality of moral feeling. This dilemma . . . is not peculiar to him." Alasdair MacIntyre, *A Short History of Ethics, Second Edition* (Notre Dame, IN: University of Notre Dame Press, 1998), 185

8 At the close of 1935, there were just two comic book publishers in the United States. They produced about ten regular titles between them. Only two of those titles, National Allied Publications' *New Fun* and *New Comics*, contained original material, and they did not sell well. Often contributing writers and artists did not receive payment for their work. Five years later, at the close of 1940, there were 23 comic book publishers

in the United States, producing at least 150 original titles, most of them spearheaded by a costumed crime-fighter. A top selling book might move more than a million copies a month, and total revenues for the industry were estimated in excess of $20 million dollars annually—perhaps $250,000,000 today—numbers that increased during the war years. In between, there was Superman. See Mike Benton, *The Comic Book In America* (Dallas, TX: Taylor Publishing Company, 1992) 14–32, *et passim* for a detailed account.

9 Gerard Jones, *Men of Tomorrow: Geeks, Gangsters, and the Birth of the Comic Book* (Cambridge, MA: Basic Books, 2004), 170.

10 Ibid.

11 Ian Gordon, *Comic Strips and Consumer Culture 1890–1945* (Washington and London: Smithsonian Institution Press, 1998), 134

12 Ibid., 139.

13 Ibid., 146.

14 Gordon's more detailed description of this process is highly recommended. See *Comic Strips and Consumer Culture*, 139–151.

15 Umberto Eco, "The Myth of Superman," in *Arguing Comics: Literary Masters on a Popular Medium*, eds. Jeet Heer and Kent Worcester (University Press of Mississippi, 2004), 164. Eco's essay was originally published in Italian in 1962, and appeared in a slightly revised English translation for the first time in 1972. Eco was therefore probably responding to the character in the earliest days of the Weisinger era. I thank Charles Hatfield for drawing my attention to this fact.

16 Patrick L. Eagan, "A Flag With a Human Face," in *Superman At Fifty*, 91.

17 *The Dark Knight Returns* remains one of the best selling graphic novels in the history of the medium, suggesting that audiences responded positively to this spectacle. Nevertheless, it would be wrong to conclude that Miller's Batman is more ethically appealing than his Superman. The Batman of *The Dark Knight Returns* is certainly "cooler" than Superman—indeed, to unpack the complexity of his appeal would require a separate essay, exploring, among other things, the place of eroticized violence within the masculine imaginary—but as an ethical figure he is not so much complex as incoherent.

18 The classic example is Jerry Siegel and Wayne Boring's moving story, "Superman's Return to Krypton," from *Superman* #141 (Nov, 1960), a time-travel tale in which Superman finds himself back on Krypton, several years before its destruction. He attends the marriage of his own parents, visits Kryptonian beauty spots such as the Rainbow Canyon, and learns many things he did not know about Kryptonian geography, society, and customs. But the joy of each discovery is bittersweet, because he knows that the planet and its culture are doomed to imminent destruction. Unable to prevent this event (since he has no powers on Krypton), Superman resolves to keep his painful knowledge secret, and to die with his family when the dark day comes; but (of course) a random accident sends him back to Earth before Krypton explodes.

This poignant story is readily interpretable in terms of the experience of traumatic loss and "survivor guilt" felt by many American Jews and

their children during the post-war years, with Krypton obviously standing for the lost Jewish traditions and communities of old Europe. While
much has been made of Superman's "Jewish origins" in recent years,
I would argue that the influence of the Jewish experience (albeit, at its
most tragic) can be felt far more strongly in this post-war tale than in any
of Siegel and Shuster's Superman comics of the 1930s and 40s including
the origin story.

19 Nowadays, many philosophers have given up the hunt for ideal principles
of justice on these grounds. For a recent and widely praised effort to
articulate principles for "comparative" rather than "transcendentalist"
ethical judgments, with some significant criticisms of Rawls, among
others, see Amartya Sen, *The Idea of Justice* (Cambridge, MA: Harvard
University Press, 2009).

20 Again, I chose this word deliberately, with an awareness that the concept
of "devotion unto excess" has been offered as a distinguishing mark of
the truly religious temper by theologians since Kierkegaard, at least.

21 This idea was perhaps most explicitly developed in a story from the 1980s,
written and drawn by one of the great auteurs of the comic book superhero genre, John Byrne. Originally published in *Superman* #2 (Feb. 1986)
and entitled "The Secret Revealed," in this tale Luthor uses a super-
computer to try and determine the nature of the connection between
Superman and Clark Kent. ("Are they friends? Cousins? Brothers?" he
asks.) When the computer tells him that Clark Kent *is* Superman, however, Luthor rejects the idea on the grounds that "no man with the
power of Superman would ever pretend to be a mere human!" The irony
is hardly subtle; but Luthor's attitude reminds us how unusual—how
unlikely—Superman's moral restraint really is.

22 *Adventure Comics* #271, "How Luthor First Met Superboy" (April, 1960).

CHAPTER TWO

1 See http://screenrant.com/megan-fox-wonder-woman-ross-10819/ for
details, or simply search online for "Megan Fox Wonder Woman."

2 This is not to say that "kick-ass" women in contemporary entertainment
media (such as Buffy or Lara Croft) have no appeal for boys. But Wonder
Woman clearly thrived in the wartime milieu of "Rosie the Riveter," and
the character has perhaps never fully recovered from the subsequent
ideological backlash.

Interestingly, the most popular female comic book superheroes of
the past 30 years, such as The Black Widow, Phoenix, Elektra, Spider-
Woman, Catwoman, and The Huntress, are moody, haunted, erratic,
and often untrustworthy: many are (partially) reformed villains. Even
Brian Michael Bendis's *Alias,* Greg Rucka's *Detective Comics*, and Gail
Simone's *Birds of Prey*—three of the best-written titles featuring
superpowered females in the last decade—do not avoid the cliché of
"super-woman with a dark side" so much as transcend it, through depth
of characterization, self-reflexive wit, and sheer stylistic brio. But Diana,

by contrast, remains noble, optimistic, and possessed of a healthy self-esteem (characteristics that can be handled without making her seem priggish or unbelievable, as both Rucka and Simone have showed). It is beyond the scope of this essay to say precisely where the bias toward gloomy female heroes comes from—whether, for example, it is a function of the nihilistic turn of the genre after the 1980s, and how assumptions about gender play out within that history. But my point is that the structures of gender identification in fantasy in the 1940s were not the same as they are today, and that it would be presentist to assume that, from a political point of view, things have only improved since those days.

3 Marc Edward DiPaolo, "Wonder Woman as World War II Veteran, Camp Feminist Icon, and Male Sex Fantasy," in *The Amazing Transforming Superhero*, ed. Terrance R. Wandtke (Jefferson NC and London: McFarland, 2007) 151.

4 It was, of course, anti-comics crusader Dr. Fredric Wertham—the greatest supervillain of them all in most comic books histories—who first condemned Wonder Woman and the Holiday Girls for their incitements to lesbianism. For a positive reading of the character in queer terms, see, for example, Brian Michael Peters, "Qu(e)erying Comic Book Culture and Representations of Sexuality In Wonder Woman," *Comparative Literature and Culture* 5: 3 (2003), an online journal from Purdue University, available at http://docs.lib.purdue.edu/clcweb.

5 Such operations of hierarchical reversal and dialectical undoing are usually declared (by their practitioners) to be intellectually and politically "productive," to the extent that they serve to displace speciously reified categories of thought. But at the same time, these acts of displacement must be acknowledged as provisional, impermanent, and incomplete, because no act of deconstruction is itself impervious to further deconstruction (indeed, many "classic" deconstructive essays of the past few decades end with a form of this assertion, in a final act of curiously confessional self-cancelling). Consequently, the intellectual and political products of deconstruction are necessarily somewhat nebulous—or dubious, depending on your level of sympathy for the business of academic theorizing. I personally consider the central insights of post-structuralism valuable and worthwhile, although I confess a measure of impatience with the literary style of much avowedly "deconstructive" criticism.

6 I take some inspiration here from Lillian S. Robinson's insight that "the female superhero begins in an act of criticism." See *Wonder Woman: Superheroes and Feminisms* (London and New York: Routledge, 2004), 7.

7 I say "too easy" because the *Bibliotheca* version actually suggests willingness on Hippolyta's part to give her belt to Hercules; he kills her in error, thanks to the actions of Hera, and sexual violence is not implied. See Pseudo-Apollodorus, *Bibliotheca*, II.v.9. (Sir James Frazer's 1921 translation is widely available online; I consulted the version at www.library.theoi.com.) By contrast, the *Bibliotheca Historica* of Diodorus Siculus (available in C. H. Oldfather's translation at the same source) positively revels in gendered violence, describing Hercules's victory over several different Amazon warriors with gleeful sarcasm. The suggestion of rape

is even stronger in certain ancient visual depictions of the event, such as the red-figure kylix attributed to Onesimos, in the British Museum.

8 Quintus of Smyrna, *The Trojan Epic: Posthomerica*, trans. Alan James (Baltimore, MD: The Johns Hopkins University Press, 2007), 20.

9 Kathryn Schwartz, *Tough Love: Amazon Encounters in the English Renaissance* (Durham and London: Duke University Press, 2000), 28.

10 Ibid., 2

11 The false etymology was itself of Greek origin, according to the *OED*. The editors of the great dictionary do not even hazard a guess as to the true source, stating only that it is probably derived "from an unknown foreign word." See *The Oxford English Dictionary*, 2ⁿᵈ ed., 1989.

12 I've drawn here from a sprightly and informative anonymous article online: http://www.straightdope.com/columns/read/2133/whats-up-with-the-amazons.

13 Schwartz, *Tough Love*, xi–ixii.

14 In the process, as Lillian Robinson notes, he also reversed "the categories of good and evil, civilization and barbarism, and by no means incidentally, male and female, as the Greek sources delineate them." See Robinson, *Wonder Women*, 31.

15 On the subject of Jews and comics, the bibliography keeps growing. Among the best are Paul Buhle's *Jews and American Comics*, (New York: New Press, 2008), Gerard Jones's *Men of Tomorrow* (New York: Basic Books, 2004), and Danny Fingeroth's *Disguised As Clark Kent: Jews, Comics, and the Creation of the Superhero* (New York and London: Continuum, 2007). For those who prefer their history as fictionalized romance, there's Michael Chabon's *The Amazing Adventures of Kavalier and Clay,* (New York: Picador, 2001).

16 For a compelling narrative about this controversial tool of modern interrogation that clearly outlines Marston's contribution, see Ken Alder, *The Lie Detectors* (New York and London: The Free Press, 2007), esp. 48–53 and 181–195. Alder's original research supplements and in some places silently amends the account of Marston's life in Les Daniels, *Wonder Woman: The Golden Age* (San Francisco: Chronicle Books, 2001). I have drawn on all both sources for this chapter, plus the pioneering article by Geoffrey C. Bunn, situating Marston's work in the historical context of his intellectual field. See Bunn, "The lie detector, Wonder Woman and liberty: the life and work of William Moulton Marston," *History of the Human Sciences,* X.i. (1997) 91–119.

17 Alder describes a piquant scene in which John Larson—a man whose claim to the title "inventor of the lie detector" was at least as good as Marston's—found himself unable to reproduce the results of Marston's initial trials in which "nine out of ten men" had supposedly expressed an "honest preference" for Gillette razors over any rival blade. Marston's campaign was about to hit the national airwaves in a series of radio commercials; Larson's report ensured this did not happen. See Alder, *The Lie Detectors*, 189–90.

18 Marston displayed significant self-awareness about his role and its precedents, describing himself to his old schoolfellow in the Harvard Class

of 1915 Twenty-fifth Anniversary Report as a "new sort of creature who seemed to combine the advisory functions of the old-time pastor and country doctor." See Bunn, "The Lie Detector," 96.

19 Having said this: Les Daniels speculates that Marston's polyamory was the reason he did not pursue a permanent position in the academy. See *Wonder Woman, The Golden Age*, 33. Marston taught as an adjunct faculty member at several institutions in the 1920s, but he does not seem to have sought tenure at any of them.

20 Cited in Alder, *The Lie Detectors*, 191.

21 Marston, "Don't Laugh at the Comics," *The Family Circle* (October 25, 1940). Most of this article is reproduced in Daniels, *Wonder Woman, The Golden Age*, 19, although not the concluding section, where Marston's fulsome praise for Gaines appears; these remarks are cited by Alder, *The Lie Detectors*, 191. For some insightful speculations about Marston's friendship with Gaines, see Jones, *Men of Tomorrow*, 205–7.

22 From Daniels, *Wonder Woman, The Golden Age*, pp. 11–12.

23 The possibility that Diana's "love" for Steve may be more a matter of his novelty than his charm is therefore implicit in the story; here we might recall Prospero's scathing remark to Miranda that, compared to others, Ferdinand is a Caliban. I'm grateful to Lara Bovilsky for drawing my attention to this parallel.

24 For an extended reading of the two versions of the origin, see Lilian S. Robinson, *Wonder Women: Feminisms and Superheroes* (New York and London: Routledge, 2004), 28–36. Marston vacillates on the question of whether the Amazons have other "god-given" children, but current continuity establishes Diana as unique. One of the best *Wonder Woman* stories of recent years, Gail Simone's *Wonder Woman: The Circle* (New York: DC Comics, 2009) explores Diana's status as the only "daughter of the Amazons."

25 I have summarized the story as reprinted in the *DC Archive Editions: Wonder Woman Archives, Vol. 1* (New York: DC Comics, 1998), 8–16.

26 The title reflects Marston's desire to appear on the fashionable edge of psychological research at that time. Where a previous generation of thinkers had tended to focus on the behavior and mental processes of social "deviants," Marston aligned himself with the movement to map the no less mysterious mechanics of the "normal" human mind.

27 William Moulton Marston, *The Emotions of Normal People* (London and New York: Kegan Paul, Trench, Trubner & Co., and Harcourt, Brace and Co., 1928).

28 Ibid., 4; Geoffrey C. Bunn, "The lie detector, Wonder Woman and liberty," 103.

29 See ibid., 91–4 and 110–15, and Alder, *The Lie Detectors*, 51–4, for positive evaluations of Marston's work in the wider history of psychology.

30 Less baldly, Marston argued that human behavior should be understood in terms of four "primary emotions," which he named dominance, submission, inducement, and compliance. Other feeling-states, such as love or fear, he labeled "compound emotions"—although to the extent that "inducement" and "compliance" constitute a further nuancing of the

notions of "dominance" and "submission," the boundary between "primary" and "compound" emotional states is less than secure from the get-go. See Marston, *Emotions,* 87–112, esp. 103–6

31 Bunn, "The lie detector, Wonder Woman and liberty," 103.

32 Marston, *Emotions,* 299–300

33 Ibid., 313. Marston is aware that his association of passion with submission runs counter to "popular parlance," but nevertheless insists: *"passion, when properly understood, suggests active submission of self to the lover"*(301, emphasis in original). His logic here is entirely circular— passion suggests submission when "properly understood" only because he has already decided that "captivation" is a better word than passion to describe dominant behavior. Adding to the confusion, he also refers to "passion emotion" as both *"passive* love" and *"active* submission." (You are probably starting to see why I described *The Emotions of Normal People* as a frustrating read.)

34 Marston, *Emotions,* 385.

35 Ibid., 328.

36 Ibid., 315–16.

37 "This appears to be the plain, emotional fact of the matter, however much dominant resistance the majority of males may feel to acknowledging that their bodies are devised for passion response, [sic] while women's bodies are devised for the capture of males and not for submission to them"(Ibid., 337). Marston attributes this natural-but-repressed male joy in submission both to the externality of the male genitals and to the pleasure of being overwhelmed by Mother, at different points in the text. But he also claims that at the moment of orgasm, men switch (for a few seconds) from "passive" to "active." This last argument is particularly convoluted, and suggests something of the difficulty Marston was having with his basic opposition of captivation and passion; thanks to the paradoxical consequences of his own theory, each keeps threatening to flip over into the other.

38 Marston's discussions of the relationship between "appetite," "desire," and "love" are some of the most elaborate in the text. At times he sounds like an American Lacan: "A formula conveniently symbolizing appetite emotion may be devised, using the formula for desire pCaD, and the formula for satisfaction aCpD, with a plus sign (+) between signifying that desire precedes and is adapted to satisfaction. . . . Since the active element of appetite is desire, it might be written aA; and since satisfaction is the passive appetitive emotion unit, it might be written pA. Appetite would not, then, be symbolized by the formula aApA but by the formula aA + pA"(Ibid., 204). Got that? However, beneath these elaborate trappings, what Marston really seems to mean by "appetite" is selfish greed, of both an emotional and materialistic variety—something the conditions of modernity seemed to him to be fostering.

39 Ibid., 338.

40 Ibid., 339.

41 Marston hedges, again, on whether woman's dual capacity for passive and active love is more physiological or psychological in origin, but seems

to lean in the direction of the former. For example, his account of the baby party ends with this speculation: "Perhaps a love hormone is operative in the female organism, predisposing girls and women to captivation emotion by evoking passive submission by intra-organic stimulation"(Ibid., 301). I confess I have no idea what Marston really means by this, but clearly biology rather than Freud is being evoked.

42 Ibid., 396. See fn. 38 for a discussion of Marston's use of the word "appetite."

43 *DC Archive Editions: Wonder Woman Archives, Vol. 1* (New York: DC Comics, 1998), 41.

44 Ibid., 37 and 44.

45 Ibid., 63.

46 Ibid., 69.

47 Bunn, 95.

48 Ibid., 91–2

49 Ibid., 134.

50 Ibid., 219. It is regrettable that the opinions of artist H. G. Peter regarding these scripts went unrecorded.

51 Douglas Wolk, *Reading Comics* (New York: Da Capo Press, 2007), 98

52 See Richard Reynolds, *Superheroes: A Modern Mythology* (Jackson, MI: University of Mississippi, 2002), 34. Reynolds does not actually cite directly from any of Marston's published works—not even from his Golden Age *Wonder Woman* comics. He bases his claim on secondary sources, and the character's "appearance and costume."

53 See Gloria Steinem, "Introduction," and other prefatory essays, *Wonder Woman* [an anthology of Marston's stories] (New York: Crown Books, 1972).

54 Trina Robbins, *The Great Women Superheroes* (Northhampton, MA: Kitchen Sink Press, 1996), 12–13.

55 *DC Archive Editions: Wonder Woman Archives* Vol. III, 111–14. The most Crumb-like panels appear on page 113. Of course, it might be argued that this kind of "escape routine" was familiar in the early twentieth century to any vaudeville audience, and I'm imposing a sexual reading on the sequence anachronistically. But I'm sure Marston would have had no problem recognizing the erotic energies of many vaudeville acts, too.

Other critics have followed Robbins, almost as if grateful to have an excuse to avoid discussing the meanings of bondage in the series. For example, somewhat incoherently, Matthew J. Smith repeats Robbins's comments approvingly before moving on to a superficial discussion of Marston's theories in "The Tyranny of the Melting Pot Metaphor: Wonder Woman as the Americanized Immigrant," *Comics and Ideology* (eds. McAllister, Sewell Jr., and Gordon), 136–37. Marc Edward DiPaolo's dispatches the discussion to a footnote, citing only Smith, Robbins, and (bizarrely, since she says nothing about the topic) Steinem.

56 Lillian S. Robinson, *Wonder Women: Superheroes and Feminism* (London and New York: Routledge, 2004), 13. See 42–45 *et passim* for her discussion of the bondage games of the Holliday girls.

57 In a generally positive article on comics (which does not explicitly mention Wonder Woman) Frank singles out "jungle adventure" strips for criticism as "fantastic and lurid," adding "magazines that exploit the female form or picture amorous embraces with the obvious purpose of stimulating sex interests are certainly not suitable for children, nor are these found among the children's favorites." Clearly, her objections to Wonder Woman were of a similar nature. See Frank, "Are Comics Bad For Children?" *Journal of Educational Psychology* (1948), XVIII: 4.

58 As cited in Daniels, 67.

59 As I have noted, it may indeed be the case that Marston got away with what he did because bondage *is* a convention of the genre; nevertheless, Marston clearly exploited the convention more self-consciously than most creators.

60 Ibid., 72, 75.

61 Even Lillian Robinson contrasts "the lesbian vibes Fredric Wertham picked up" with "Marston's vision of female power based on kittenish heterosexuality." She supports these claims with appropriate passages from interviews with Marston himself, but does not consider his remarks about female sexuality in his academic work. See Robinson, *Wonder Women*, 52–3.

62 This is not to say that Marston should be thought of in contemporary progressive political terms. His attitudes were shaped by what he saw as "scientific facts" (however dubious they may now seem to us) rather than by a late liberal concern with individual rights and freedoms; and those "facts" led him to make a quite different prognosis with regard to male-male relationships—although even here, as elsewhere, he could be seen as vacillating. The point to be grasped is that Wonder Woman was consciously conceived as part of an "intellectual struggle over hegemonic norms" *vis-à-vis* female sexuality, as Molly Rhodes puts it in "Wonder Woman and Her Disciplinary Powers: The Queer Intersection of Scientific Authority and Mass Culture," in *Doing Science and Culture*, eds. Roddey Reid and Sharon Traweek (New York and London: Routledge, 2000), 115. Rhodes's "theoretical" prose can be wince-inducing (e.g., "Traces of Wonder Woman's early discursive build [sic] persist within the first production period of the comic, 1941–48"); but her essentially Foucauldian effort to place Marston's use of "science" within the context of the cultural battle to establish norms of sexual morality does suggest the potential complexity of the issues involved. She also draws our attention to a patronizing attack on Marston by Cleanth Brooks and Robert Heilman, passed over by most other commentators. But she overstates Marston's debt to neurology, and the final point of her work isn't clear, even in her own telling: "Noting a complementary agenda for cultural studies of science, technology, and medicine and for queer theory because of science and medicine's pervasive presence in modern sexuality, I argue for the treatment and instrumental use [sic] of queer theory within a larger trajectory of intellectual and cultural history, and emphasize that an interdisciplinary cultural history of psychology is crucial for the

advancement of our knowledge of modern sexuality"(97). The intersection of Marston's theories for contemporary queer theory in general, and for queer readings of Wonder Woman in particular, could be the subject of a separate essay; and despite its shortcomings, Rhodes's work provides a good place to start.

63 Ken Alder discovered this manuscript in the collection of Marston Family Papers held by Margaret Lampe; I am enormously grateful to him for sharing the fruits of his research, and to Ms. Lampe for her willingness to share these papers with the scholarly community.

64 I could cite a very long list of books and articles containing a bewildering range of opinions on the appropriately "feminist" stance toward bondage and other forms of alternative sexual practice and fantasy. In place of them all, I will simply recommend Laura Kipnis's *Bound and Gagged: The Politics of Pornography in America* (Durham and London: Duke University Press, 1999) for a series of essays that parse out the complex relationship between sexual fantasies and social politics with intelligence and style.

65 *The Greatest Wonder Woman Stories Ever Told* (New York: DC Comics, 2007), 56.

66 Sarah Coakley, *Powers and Submissions: Spirituality, Philosophy, and Gender* (Oxford: Blackwell, 2002), xii.

67 Ibid., xiv. Coakley cites Karl Barth, Hans Urs von Balthasar, and Jurgen Moltmann in this context.

68 Ibid., xv.

69 Ibid., 3.

70 Ibid., 5.

71 Ibid., 34–5

72 Ibid., xii.

73 I anticipate reading her own direct engagement with these issues in her long anticipated forthcoming work on the subject.

74 John Donne, "Elegy XIX: To His Mistress Going to Bed," in *Complete English Poems*, ed. A. J. Smith (London: Penguin Books, 1996), 125.

75 The great exception here is Greg Rucka, who consciously revised Marston's themes of dominance and submission for a modern audience in what are some of the best *Wonder Woman* stories since the 1940s. For example, *The Hiketeia* (New York: DC Comics, 2002), illustrated by J. G. Jones, explores the notion of "topping-from-the-bottom," basing several turns of the plot upon Wonder Woman's participation as the dominant party in an ancient Greek ritual of service. Unfortunately, in one of the more incomprehensible editorial decisions at DC in recent years, Rucka was taken off the *Wonder Woman* title in the middle of his exceptional run, leaving several plot threads dangling—despite improving sales and terrific critical notices—for an ill-conceived re-boot of the character by Allan Heinberg. Widely regarded as a disaster, Heinberg's arc was followed by an equally disappointing story by Jodi Picoult (whose brief tenure on the book was also marred by editorial mandates). It was only when the book was placed in the hands of Gail Simone, more than

two years later, that Wonder Woman found her feet again. Simone undid a great deal of damage, and restored some of Diana's lost prestige. However, at the time of this writing, Wonder Woman has been subjected to yet another makeover, with a new creative team, a new origin (eliminating much of what is distinctive about the character), and a new costume. Fan reaction thus far has been scathing.

In a recent online interview, Rucka spoke interestingly about the difficulties of writing and marketing Wonder Woman: "Feminism is a shifting concept and she is inherently a political character. If you are a corporate entity like DC/Warner Brothers, that is immediately problematic. The options seem to be, either write her as Superman but female, or try to embrace what makes her Wonder Woman, and I think that for the most part the attempts to embrace . . . get met on a corporate level with a certain resistance." I find some support for my own reading of the character as inherently deconstructive in Rucka's perceptive remarks. See http://www.comicbookdaily.com/wp/blogs/diary-of-a-comic-book-goddess-the-greg-rucka-interview/ for more.

76 I write about the split between sexuality and the sacred as a defining feature of modernity in my previous book, *Desiring Donne: Poetry, Sexuality, Interpretation* (Cambridge, MA: Harvard University Press, 2006) 51–6, *et passim*.

CHAPTER THREE

1 Stan Lee and Steve Ditko, "Spider-Man!" in *Amazing Fantasy* #15 (August, 1962), 8.

2 See Mark Evanier's useful blog entry at http://www.newsfromme.com/archives/2005_10_06. html.

3 Some may see my application of trauma theory to a comic book character and his readers as further evidence that "the concept of trauma has become debased currency," as Ruth Leys writes in *Trauma: A Genealogy* (Chicago: University of Chicago Press, 2000), 2. However, as Leys' own study shows, the slippage between traumatic experience and traumatic representation constitutes a fundamental paradox at the heart of any serious attempt to understand the concept. Moreover, as Elisabeth Bronfen observes: "It seems as necessary to stress the . . . difference between real violence done to a physical body and an 'imagined' one . . . as it is necessary to explore the ways in which these two registers become conflated and confused." See Elisabeth Bronfen, *Over Her Dead Body: Death, Femininity, and the Aesthetic* (New York: Routledge, 1992), 59. Without claiming that the trauma experienced by the characters in an artwork, or by the audience of that artwork, is somehow the same as that experienced by a victim of real-world violence, I am intrigued by the structural similarities of response that arise despite that irreducible difference; ultimately, I am interested in what those similarities suggest about the origins of both desire and anxiety.

4 Sigmund Freud, *Standard Edition of the Complete Psychological Works*, ed. James Strachey, Vol. 18 (London: The Hogarth Press, 1955), 16.

5 Although he does not cite Freud, Lawrence Watt-Evans has explored this aspect of Peter's traumatic response to Uncle Ben's death, contrasting it with Batman's very different reaction to the death of his parents. See "Peter Parker's Penance," in *Webslinger: Unauthorized Essays on Your Friendly Neighborhood Spider-Man*, ed. Gerry Conway (Dallas, TX: Benbella Books, 2006), 17–24.

6 Freud, *SE*, Vol. XVIII, 18.

7 Freud's theory of trauma raises obvious questions about our conception of memory. The repetitive symptom turns out, somewhat paradoxically, to be the manifestation of an unconscious memory or unbearable knowledge—that is, a memory we have forgotten we remember, or a knowledge that we don't know we know. To be free of its grip, and of the attendant compulsively repeated behaviors or thoughts, we must remember what we have forgotten in order to forget it properly again. But as strange as this paradox sounds, pop-culture has long been able to handle it; witness the title of one of Elvis Presley's early hits, "I Forgot to Remember to Forget."

8 Stan Lee, John Romita, Sr., and Sal Buscema, *The Amazing Spider-Man*, #94 (March, 1971), 6.

9 Stan Lee and Steve Ditko, *The Amazing Spider-Man* #1 (March, 1963), 14.

10 Stan Lee and Steve Ditko, *The Amazing Spider-Man* #4 (September, 1963), 21.

11 Stan Lee, Gil Kane, and Frank Giacoia, *The Amazing Spider-Man*, #100 (Aug., 1971), 18. Peter then wakes to discover that the serum he has taken had the opposite effect than the one intended. Instead of removing his powers, it has made him more spider-like than ever, causing him to grow four extra arms—rendering him truly monstrous. The irony is thus pressed home further; in his effort to escape from his Spider-Man identity Peter has become more spider than man. He reverts back to his "normal" state in the following issues, of course.

12 Variants on this phrase are common in Beckett's writing; perhaps most famously, it is the final sentence of his novel, *The Unnamable*.

13 The experiment proved tremendously successful in the short term, allowing for levels of character development previously unheard of in the superhero genre; but over the longer term, it created obvious problems. Fans expected their favorite hero to continue to grow and mature, but the conventions of the adventure serial placed a practical limit on just how old Peter could credibly become. Thus, while it took less than 3 (real time) years for Peter to graduate from high school, it took almost 13 years for him to graduate from college (in #185), and his aging process was further retarded from that point on. True continuity buffs could probably argue that Peter aged approximately 15 years in the first 40 or so years of *The Amazing Spider-Man*, making him 32 or so at his oldest. In the current Marvel Universe, the clock has been reset, by means of the rather

unsatisfactory expedient of demonic "magic." Today, Peter appears to be a somewhat immature 25 year old.

14 These aspects of her personality would not survive Ditko's sudden and much mythologized departure from the comic, with #38. But having said that, it is not easy to imagine how her relationship with Peter could have progressed if Ditko had stayed. Under Ditko's direction, Gwen's ambivalent interest in Peter is mostly a matter of piqued vanity (distracted by his problems, he does not pay attention to her the way other men do); and at the end of the day, she just doesn't seem the type of girl to end up with a penniless nerd who lives with his Aunt, no matter what reserves of inner dignity she might sense within him. The idea of Ditko's Gwen pairing up with Ditko's Peter finally seems about as likely as Katherine Hepburn in the *The Philadelphia Story* choosing Jimmy Stewart over Cary Grant.

15 Romita's remarks in a later interview suggest he saw Mary Jane as providing that certain something that was missing from the Peter-Gwen dynamic: "Gwen never would have noticed Peter if Mary Jane hadn't started throwing herself at him." See Tom DeFalco, *Comics Creators on Spider-Man* (London: Titan Books, 2004), 32.

16 DeFalco, *Comics Creators*, 46.

17 As he later told Tom DeFalco: "[the Lee/Ditko comics had] the feeling I wanted to recreate. [And] Ditko . . . liked to torture his characters." Ibid.

18 Gerry Conway, Gil Kane, and John Romita Sr., *The Amazing Spider-Man* #121 (June, 1973), 12–16.

19 Ibid., 18–19.

20 According to Bronfen, the overdetermined image of the beautiful female victim always figures the act of artistic creation. Consequently, "the death of a beautiful woman marks the *mise en abyme* of a text, the moment of self-reflexivity, where the text seems to comment on itself and its own process of composition, and so decomposes itself." See *Over Her Dead Body*, 71.

21 For an argument to this effect, see Arnold T. Blumberg, "The Night Gwen Stacy Died: The End of Innocence and the Birth of the Bronze Age," a paper presented at the Comics Arts Conference, July 20–23, 2006, San Diego, and published online by *Reconstruction: Studies in contemporary culture* (Fall 2003:v. 3, no. 4). See http://reconstruction.eserver.org/034/blumberg.htm.

22 Cathy Caruth, "Introduction," *Trauma: Explorations In Memory,* ed. Caruth (Baltimore MD: Johns Hopkins University Press, 1995), 5.

23 DeFalco, *Comics Creators*, 47–48.

24 One can hardly blame Stan and Gerry for making this appeal, given the intensity of some readers' reactions. As Conway put it, many years later: "The fans wanted to throw me off a bridge, too. The hatred was so intense I stopped going to conventions for a while." See http://forcesofgood.com/2008/05/15/5-questions-gerry-conway/

25 Gerry Conway, Gil Kane, and John Romita, Sr., *The Amazing Spider-Man* #122 (July, 1973), 7, 19.

26 Gerry Conway, Gil Kane, and John Romita, Sr., *The Amazing Spider-Man* #123 (August, 1973), 8.

27 Gerry Conway, Gil Kane, and John Romita, Sr., *The Amazing Spider-Man* #124, (September, 1973), 13.

28 My phrasing here follows that of Frederick Sontag's essay, "Repetition/ Freedom," in *A Kierkegaard Handbook* (U.S.A.: John Knox Press, 1979), 119.

29 See, for example, Slavoj Zizek, "Why Is Every Act a Repetition?" in *Enjoy Your Symptom* (New York and London: Routledge, 1992), 82–86.

30 Søren Kierkegaard, *Either/Or*, Vol. II. trans. David F. Swenson and Lilian Marvin Swenson (Garden City, NY: Doubleday, 1959), 173.

31 Søren Kierkegaard, *The Sickness Unto Death*, trans. Walter Lowrie (Garden City, NY: Doubleday, 1954), 153.

32 To elaborate: in the encounter with existential absurdity, both Kierkegaard and Spider-Man are forced to confront the fact that there are no objective or absolute standards upon which to ground moral choices. In the absence of an external court-of-appeal that can assess the virtue of our decisions, morality is therefore at the end of the day a matter of individual choice. Hegellians will note here that category of the aesthetic is not so much escaped via the ethical as sublated within the ethical. To render the point in non-Hegelese, if morality is recognized to be a personal choice, then the supposed distinction between the ethical and the aesthetic may not be as firm as it first appeared; in other words, for Kierkegaard, to affirm the religious may be, in a complex way, to affirm the ethical as a special form of aesthetics.

33 Søren Kierkegaard, *Fear and Trembling*, eds. C. Stephen Evans and Sylvia Walsh, trans. Walsh (Cambridge: Cambridge University Press, 2006) 67.

34 Alisdair MacIntyre, *A Short History of Ethics* (Notre Dame, IN: University of Notre Dame Press, 1998), 218. For a brief discussion of MacIntyre's more substantive and hugely influential account of Kierkegaard in *After Virtue*, see 153n17.

35 John D. Caputo, *On Religion* (London and New York: Routledge, 2001), 50.

36 Here a passage from the French Catholic writer, Georges Bernanos, seems particularly apt: "Christians aren't supermen, [and] saints [are] still less [superhuman] since they are the most human of human beings. Saints are not sublime, they have no need of the sublime; it is rather the sublime that needs them. Saints are not heroes in the manner of Plutarch's heroes. A hero gives the illusion of surpassing humanity. The saint doesn't surpass it, he assumes it, he strives to realize [his or her] humanity in the best possible way . . . He [or she] strives to approach as nearly as possible his model, Jesus Christ, that is, to come as close as possible to him who was the perfect man, with a simplicity so perfect that in reassuring others he disconcerts the hero; for Christ did not die only for heroes—he died for cowards too." See "Our Friends the Saints," in *The Last Essays of Georges Bernanos*, trans. by Joan and Barry Ulanov (Chicago: Henry Regnery Company, 1955). I'm grateful to Professor Ralph C. Wood for drawing my attention to Bernanos's work.

37 Kierkegaard, *Fear and Trembling*, 14. Of course, Spider-Man's irrationality does not have quite the scandalous character that Kierkegaard attributes

to Abraham—it does not violate conventional ethics in the same striking way. But Kierkegaard also offers Job as another example of an authentically religious attitude, and an "exemplar for all humankind." On this topic, see Mark Lloyd Taylor, "Ordeal and Repetition in Kierkegaard's Treatment of Abraham and Job," in *The Foundation of Kierkegaard's Vision of Community* ed. George B. Connell and C. Stephan Evans (New Jersey: Humanities Press, 1992), and Edward F. Mooney, "Kierkegaard's Job Discourse: Getting Back the World," in *The Philosophy of Religion* 34 (1993), 151–69. It should be easy to see why Spider-Man is the most Job-like of superheroes.

38 Bronfen, *Over Her Dead Body*, xi.

39 Thomas Pfau, *Romantic Moods: Paranoia, Trauma, and Melancholy, 1790–1840* (Baltimore: Johns Hopkins University Press, 2005), 193.

40 Caruth, *Trauma*, 5.

41 The death of Jason Todd, the second Robin, doesn't even come close.

42 Jonathan Lethem, "Who's Afraid of Dr. Strange?" *Bookforum* (Summer, 2001). For a better than average blog entry, see Bully's "I Love Gwen Stacy" at http://blog.newsarama.com/links/?p=4179. Gwen is also perhaps the only comic book character to have her own virtual shrine, where fans can gather to venerate her memory (see www.gwenstacyshrine.tk.). Other fan sites and forums will be cited where relevant, but I invite the genuinely curious reader simply to Google the name "Gwen Stacy."

43 Other aspects of Conway's *Spectacular* run were more successful; the political subtext of his immigration themed stories, and his handling of Mary Jane's cousin's bulimia, are particularly noteworthy.

44 I will spare readers an attempt to explain the garbled and convoluted epic story line known as "The Clone Saga" that dominated Spider-Man's many comics during the 1990s. But the complaint that the creators themselves no longer cared during this period is belied by the fact that even a flawed epic like the Clone Saga culminates with an attempt to heal the greatest wound in the psyche of the Spider-Man character. In its final pages, the clone-Gwen (no longer Joyce Delaney) falls, like the original Gwen, from a great height; and this time, instead of trying to catch her with a web-line, Peter swings down to catch her, saving her life.

45 Brian Michael Bendis and Oliver Coipel, *House of M* (New York: Marvel Comics, 2008).

46 Jeph Loeb and Tim Sale, *Spider-Man: Blue* (New York: Marvel Comics, 2004).

47 J. Michael Straczynski and Mike Deodato, *The Amazing Spider-Man Volume Eight: Sins Past* (New York: Marvel Comics, 2005)

48 For an example of the last kind, see J. R. Fettingers' exhaustive (and somewhat exhaustingly symptomatic) essay, "Deflowering Gwen," at http://www.spideykicksbutt.com. (Spiderfans who wish to check any detail of the continuity could do worse than visit Fettingers useful website.) For examples of the first two reactions, and counterarguments, simply perform an online search for the phrases "Gwen Stacy slut" or "Gwen Stacy whore."

49 Writing at comic book website *Newsarama*, Straczynski claimed that he regretted *Sins Past*, and hoped to undo it at the end of his run on Spider-Man: "I wanted to retcon the Gwen twins out of continuity, which was something I always assumed I could do at the end of my run. I wasn't allowed to do this, and yes, it pissed me off. I felt I was left holding the bag for something I wanted to get rid of, and taking the rap for a writing lapse that I had never committed." See http://forum.newsarama.com/showthread.php?t=141756

50 The pioneer figure in post-Freudian elaborations of the pre-oedipal stage is, of course, Melanie Klein; but the topic is central to influential works of feminist theory such as Nancy Chodorow's *The Reproduction of Mothering* (Berkeley: University of California Press, 1978) and Jessica Benjamin's *The Bonds of Love* (New York: Pantheon, 1988).

51 Janet Adelman, *Suffocating Mothers* (New York and London: Routledge, 1992), 125.

52 Ibid., 126.

53 Ibid.

CHAPTER FOUR

1 Donna Haraway, "A Cyborg Manifesto," *The Harraway Reader* (New York and London: Routledge, 2004), 8.

2 Stan Lee and Don Heck, *Tales of Suspense* #46, esp. pp. 1, 2, 8, and 13. Reprinted in *The Essential Iron Man Volume One* (New York: Marvel Comics, 2000).

3 This is the fate of Drexel Cord in *The Invincible Iron Man* #2, The Unicorn in #4, the Crusher in #8, The Controller in #12, and many others.

4 Although Goodwin's story does not attempt to describe a scientifically accurate scenario for his disaster, this is surely one of the earliest warnings about the "feedback" effect of climate change in American pop culture.

5 Archie Goodwin and Johnny Craig, *The Invincible Iron Man* #25 (May, 1970), as reprinted in *Marvel Omnibus: The Invincible Iron Man Volume II* (New York: Marvel Comics, 2010), 797818.

6 Bill Mantlo and George Tuska, *The Invincible Iron Man* #78, 3, 14, 17, 2. Iron Man's gradual shift away from strident anticommunism to a less conservative posture is also charted by Bradford Wright in *Comic Book Nation* (Baltimore, MA: Johns Hopkins University Press), 241–43, but Wright does not discuss the issue of techno-ambivalence.

7 Kate Soper, *Humanism and Anti-Humanism* (London: Open Court Publishing Company, 1986), 14, 15

8 See the Introduction to this book for a more detailed discussion of Neiman's work.

9 Susan Neiman, *Evil In Modern Thought: An Alternative History of Philosophy* (Princeton and Oxford: Princeton University Press, 2002), 99. My discussion here is much indebted to Neiman's remarkable book.

10 Ibid., 95.

11 Ibid., 85.

12 Brent Waters, *From Human to Posthuman* (Aldershot and Burlington: Ashgate, 2006), 13.

13 Ibid., 21.

14 Neiman puts it slightly differently, writing that "humankind lost faith in the world at Lisbon, and faith in itself at Auschwitz." See Neiman, *Evil,* 250.

15 N. Katherine Hayles, *How We Became Posthuman* (London and Chicago: The University of Chicago Press, 1999), 3.

16 This analogy may also help to illustrate the philosophical limit of the posthuman vision; for how, finally, can we distinguish the supposedly extraneous effects of materialization from the primary "information" that is regarded as essential to the experience of the music? Eliminating tape hiss might seem reasonable enough, but what about the noise of a musician's fingers squeaking on a fret-board, or foot-tapping, or breathing or humming, or even the unique ambience of the room or concert hall in which the song was first "materialized"? To put it another way, the problem with the posthuman prioritizing of information over matter is that it assumes the existence of a clearly discernible line between form and content. But as any reader of poetry knows, at any level that matters, form and content are indivisible. The notion that the body is merely the container of information that could be transferred, without significant loss or change, into some other container, is therefore not merely wildly speculative— it is aesthetically impoverished.

17 Ray Kurzweil, *The Singularity Is Near: When Humans Transcend Biology* (London and New York: Penguin, 2005), 375.

18 See, for example, the essays in Neil Badmington's *Alien Chic: Posthumanism and the Other Within* (New York and London: Routledge, 2004).

19 See Anthony Miccoli, *Posthuman Suffering and the Technological Embrace* (Plymouth: Lexington Books, 2010), 4–8 for a critique of Hayles's liberalism.

20 Archie Goodwin and Johnny Craig, *The Invincible Iron Man* #2 (June, 1968), reprinted in *Marvel Omnibus: The Invincible Iron Man Volume II* (New York: Marvel Comics, 2010), 288.

21 David Michelinie, John Romita, Jr, and Bob Layton, *Iron Man: Demon in a Bottle* (New York: Marvel Comics, 2008 [reprinting material first published in 1979]), 155.

22 Roget Lockard, "Self-Will Run Riot: The Earth As n Alcoholic," in *Janus Head* VI: 2 (2003), 193, 195.

23 By the 1980s, this had changed. Suffering an alcoholic relapse, Stark loses everything—his company, his friendships, and his Iron Man identity. His good friend Rhodey Rhodes takes over the role in *Iron Man* #170, and remained inside the armor for the next two years, while Tony took the necessary time to make a more complete recovery.

24 The relevant steps read as follows: "1. We admitted we were powerless over alcohol—that our lives had become unmanageable." "5. Admitted to God, to ourselves, and to another human being the exact nature of

our wrongs." "9. Made direct amends to such people wherever possible, except when to do so would injure them or others."

25 David Michelinie, Mark Bright, and Bob Layton, *Armor Wars* (New York: Marvel Comics, 2010 [reprints material first published in 1987]).

26 Ibid., 143–144.

27 Lockard, "Self-Will," 194–195.

28 Warren Ellis and Adi Granov, *Iron Man: Extremis* (New York: Marvel Comics, 2007). The pages of this text are, unfortunately, not numbered.

29 A similar exchange takes place between Tony and a pretty *Vanity Fair* reporter in the first *Iron Man* movie—indeed, the movie is more obviously influenced by the Ellis/Granov conception of the character, in both dialog and design. But Ellis's Tony Stark has none of the cocky self-assurance of Robert Downey Jr's, and the conversation in the film takes place before Tony is wounded by one of his own weapons in Afghanistan, while the Pillinger interview takes place afterward. Overall, the effect of the comic is more subtle and complex; where Tony's crisis of faith in the movie is represented as an awakening to the immorality of arms dealing, in Ellis's *Extremis*, Tony is also increasingly uncertain about his role as a technologist, and concerned that Pillinger's assessment of the Iron Man armor might even be right.

30 To be clear: How we respond to our feelings may indeed be a matter of will. But the feelings themselves are not. Outside of an addictive cycle, we don't get to choose to feel happy, sad, jealous, proud, or angry; only our reactions to those feelings could be called a matter of choice. (Assuming one believes in the currently philosophically unfashionable notion of free will, that is.)

31 Leslie H. Farber, *Lying, Despair, Jealousy, Envy, Sex, Suicide, Drugs, and the Good Life*, (New York: Basic Books, 1976), 117–18. Farber is an amazing writer, and is currently more neglected in academic circles than he should be.

32 Ibid., 6, 7.

33 Ibid., 118–19.

34 Given that Bill Wilson's writings for AA have probably now been read with more care by more people than the works of Marx, Hegel, and Freud, combined, the curious failure of the academy to engage seriously with 12 step theory is itself a question worthy of investigation.

35 See the introduction to this book for a short discussion of the attractions, and limitations, of postmodern theology, at least as expressed in the writings of John D. Caputo. The crucial move away from dogmatism in AA comes in the Third Step, which emphasizes the importance of turning one's life over to "God as we understand Him" (or "God as we understand God" as some other 12 Step groups prefer—avoiding the sexist assumptions of the gendered pronoun). With this five word phrase, the founders of AA released all future members from any particular idea of God or religion—while simultaneously suggesting that participants should develop their own understanding of a "power greater than themselves" upon which to rely.

36 See Ernest Kurtz, *Not-God: A History of Alcoholics Anonymous* [Expanded Edition] (Center City, MN: Hazleden, 1991), esp. 3–4, 35–36, 205–07.
37 Ibid., 182.
38 Ibid., 209.
39 Anonymous, *Alcoholics Anonymous "Big Book"* [Fourth Edition] (Alcoholics Anonymous World Service, 2001), 62.
40 Kurtz, *Not-God*, p. 205.
41 Ibid., 206.
42 Tony Davies, *Humanism* (New York and London: Routledge, 2008), 140. Davies's book is a good entry point into the meanings of this much-abused term.

CODA

1 For a very fine essay on this topic, see the last chapter of Scott Bukatman's *Matters of Gravity* (Durham and London: Duke University Press, 2003).

APPENDIX

1 See, for example, Martin Barker, *A Haunt of Fears: The Strange History of the British Horror Comics Campaign* (Jackson and London: University Press of Mississippi, 1992); Jose Alaniz, *Komiks: Comic Art in Russia* (Jackson and London: University Press of Mississippi, 2010); *Natso Onodo Power, God of Comics: Osamu Tezuka and the Creation of Post-World War II Manga* (Jackson and London: University Press of Mississippi, 2009).
2 In 2009, Randy Duncan and Matthew J. Smith produced the first textbook specifically designed for this fledging discipline, entitled *The Power of Comics: History, Form and Culture* (New York and London: Continuum, 2009).
3 One example might be the notion of the "ages" of the American comic book—the Golden Age, Silver Age, Bronze Age, and so on. With some reservations, I have continued to deploy these terms in my work on super-heroes because I believe it is reasonable—or at least defensible—to see the first 35 years or so of the superhero genre as made up of two more-or-less distinct historical periods, marked by recognizably different artistic conventions (with the shift occurring at some point in the early 1950s). However, it is less apparent that the concepts of the "Golden" and "Silver" ages really tell us much about the development of other forms and genres; indeed, when it comes to the thinking about the peri-odization of comics history in a less generically specific way, the "ages" may be more misleading than informative as categories, and require refinement or abandonment.
4 On this topic, see also Charles Hatfield, *Alternative Comics: An Emergent Literature* (Jackson: University Press of Mississipi, 2005), xiii.

5 The list can be found at more than one online location. I last consulted it here: http://en.academic.ru/dic.nsf/enwiki/159368.

6 See, if you must, John Shelton Lawrence and Robert Jewett, *The Myth of the American Superhero* (Grand Rapids, MI: William B. Eerdmans, 2002).

7 Jeffrey A. Brown, *Black Superheroes, Milestone Comics, and Their Fans* (Jackson and London: University Press of Mississippi, 2001), 100.

8 Lillian S. Robinson has also commented on the lack of interest in comics displayed by most high-profile scholars of mass media and cultural studies. See *Wonder Women: Feminisms and Superheroes* (London and New York: Routledge, 2004), 2. Henry Jenkins is something of an exception, here. I would also unhesitatingly recommend Brown's book, Bradford W. Wright's *Comic Book Nation* (Baltimore, MA: Johns Hopkins University Press), and Ian Gordon's *Comic Strips and Consumer Culture, 1890–1945* (Washington and London: Smithsonian Institution Press, 1998) for work on comics in the cultural studies vein.

9 A simple online search will quickly demonstrate the disproportionate attention paid to these creators in such established academic journals as *Modern Fiction Studies, Contemporary Fiction, Women's Studies Quarterly,* and *PMLA*. My point is not, by the way, that this academic work is weak—on the contrary, some of it is very good indeed—much less that Bechdel, et al., are not worthy of attention. But if your only tool is "ideology critique," every text can look like a problem in identity politics. The academic focus on autobiographical graphic novels can also serve to perpetuate the notion that comics only became suitable objects of study with the emergence of the "graphic novel" as a commercial form—a historically ignorant position that in the long run will do the discipline of Comics Studies far more harm than good.

10 I'm grateful to Charles Hatfield for sharpening my sense of the distinction between academic comics scholars and the aesthetic criteria of *The Comics Journal* in the course of a helpful e-mail exchange. Again, I'm not suggesting that the boundaries of these communities are fixed or impermeable; there are academic scholars who have published on genre comics in the pages of the *Journal* itself, after all.

11 See Peter Coogan, *Superhero: The Secret Origins of a Genre* (Austin, TX: Monkey Brain, 2006); Danny Fingeroth's *Superman on the Couch* (New York and London: Continuum, 2004); Robin Rosenberg (ed.), *The Psychology of Superheroes* (Dallas, TX: BenBella Books, 2008); Gerard Jones, *Men of Tomorrow* (New York: Basic Books, 2004); Lillian S. Robinson, *Wonder Women: Feminisms and Superheroes* (New York and London: Routledge, 2004). On Batman, see for example, Will Brooker's *Batman Unmasked* (New York and London: Continuum, 2001); Roberta E. Pearson and William Uricchio, *The Many Lives of the Batman* (New York and London: Routledge, 1991).

12 Beaty's work as both a critic and translator should be brought to the attention of all superhero scholars. *Fredric Wertham and the Critique of Mass Culture* (Jackson and London: University Press of Mississippi, 2007) has forever complicated our perceptions of one of the most hated

figures in comic book history, and his discussion of modernism and postmodernism in *Unpopular Culture: Transforming the European Comic Book in the 1990s* (London, Buffalo, Toronto: University of Toronto Press, 2007) broaches some of the same issues I am raising here—albeit in a far more overtly theoretical register— with regard to the European tradition. Charles Hatfield's *Alternative Comics: An Emerging Literature* (Jackson and London: University Press of Mississippi, 2005) is filled with intelligent and perspicacious close readings. His forthcoming book on Jack Kirby will also surely be required reading. Kannenberg Jr's "The Comics of Chris Ware: Text, Image, and Visual Narrative Strategies," appears in *The Language of Comics*, eds. Varnum and Gibbons (Jackson and London: University Press of Mississippi, 2001). Joseph Witek's *Comic Books as History: The Narrative Art of Jack Jackson, Art Spiegelman, and Harvey Pekar* (Jackson and London: University Press of Mississippi, 1989), the oldest of the works listed here, remains valuable for all comics scholars—not just critics of the artists named in the subtitle. There are, of course, many other fine critics working in the larger field, and I hope no one will feel slighted if they are not named here.

13 See Douglas Wolk, *Reading Comics* (Da Capo Press, 2007), 89–117, esp. 92–93.

14 The exception here is the work of Scott Bukatman, whose essays on superheroes in *Matters of Gravity* (Durham and London: Duke University Press, 2003) attempt to articulate a "phenomenology" of superhero comics, exploring the ways in which the genre exploits the visual to engage fantasies of enhanced embodiment. It's terrific stuff.

15 Here I have in mind a recent essay by Hillary Chute, "Comics as Literature: Reading Graphic Narrative," *PMLA* 123:2(2008) 452–65. Chute describes autobiographical comics as the "strongest" work in the medium in her first pages, and dismisses "mainstream" comics in a parenthetical aside. Chute is a fine reader of her chosen creators, and has worked to increase the profile of Comics Studies at the MLA by lobbying for a discussion group—all things I strongly applaud—but her imposition of a dubious hierarchy of value upon categories of generic distinction illustrates precisely the critical tendency that I hope we can avoid, as the field continues to grow.

INDEX

Abraham 12, 93–5
Adelman, Janet 101–2
Alaniz, José 172n1
Alcoholics Anonymous, Spirituality
　of 135–40
Alder, Ken 158n16, 158n17, 163n63
Allred, Michael 96
Amazons, significations of
　the 39–41, 44–5
Andru, Ross 97
Aristotle 30
Armstrong, Louis 19
Augustine, Saint 2

Barry, Lynda 148
Batman 25, 27, 36, 44, 79, 80,
　155n17
Battaille, Georges 65
Beatles, The 14, 19
Beaty, Bart 150, 173n12
Bechdel, Allison 145, 148
Beckett, Samuel 79
Bendis, Brian Michael 96, 98, 145
Bernanos, Georges 167n36
Bonhoeffer, Dietrich 12
Boring, Wayne 155n18
Bronfen, Elisabeth 95, 164n3
Brooker, Will 173n10
Brown, Jeffrey A. 147
Bukatman, Scott 152n2, 172n1,
　174n14
Bunn, Geoffrey C. 46
Busiek, Kurt 96
Byrne, John 156n21

Campbell, Joseph 16
Captain Marvel 1, 58
Caputo, John 8–11, 153n16
Carruth, Cathy 87, 96
children's literature 7–8
Christ, Jesus 14, 16, 17
　vulnerability of 66–7
Christianity 9–11, 32, 65, 73, 93–4,
　135, 155
　and feminism 66–70
Churchill, Winston 12
Chute, Hillary 174n15
Coakley, Sarah 39, 66–70
Cole, Jack 146
Comics Journal, The 146, 148
Conway, Gerry 83–5, 87–90, 95,
　96–8
Coogan, Peter 149
Craig, Johnny 111
Crumb, Robert 58
cyborg sex 105–6

Daniels, Les 58–60
Daredevil 81, 83
David, Peter 96
Davis, Alan 1
deconstruction 10–11, 37–8, 143,
　146, 157n5
Deodato, Mike 96, 99
Derrida, Jacques 14
DiPaolo, Marc Edward 37
Ditko, Steve 75, 80, 81–2, 84, 95,
　148, 166n14
Donne, John 69